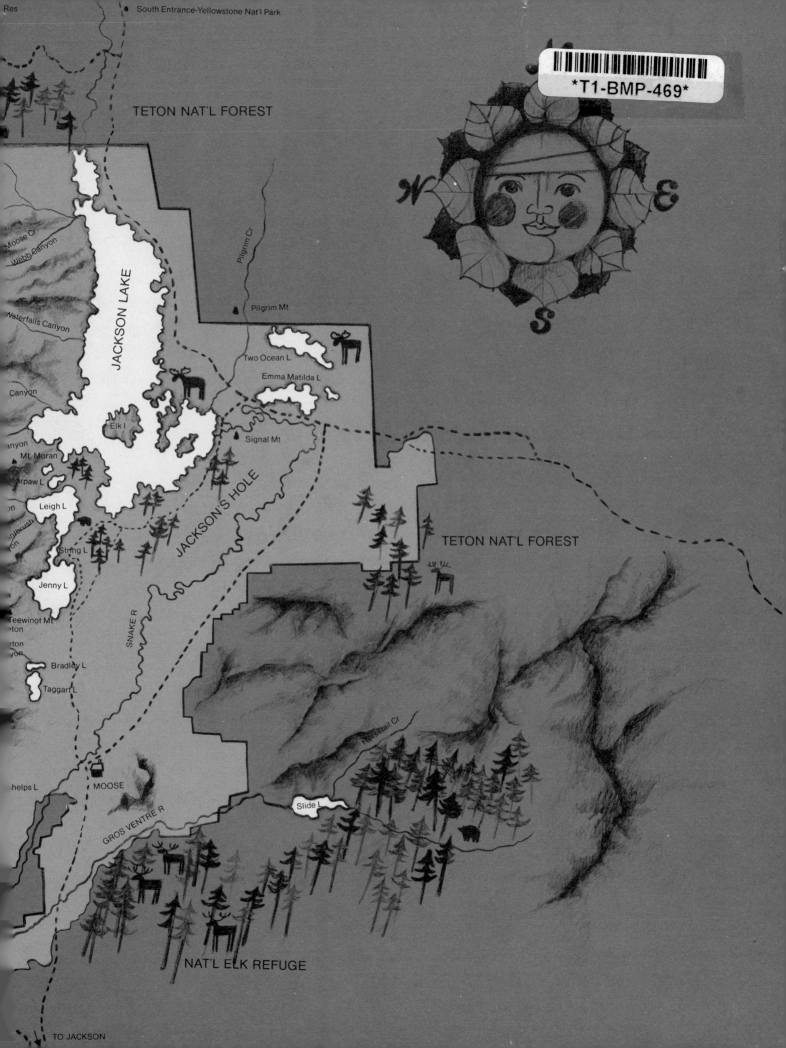

THE GRAND TETONS

THE GRAND

A Studio Book   THE VIKING PRESS

TETONS

Boyd Norton

New York

To Barbara, who shared a great deal of this

Design: Christopher Holme
Endpaper map by Julie B. Sliker, Design Associates, Evergreen,
Colorado

First published in 1974 by The Viking Press, Inc.
625 Madison Avenue, New York, N.Y. 10022

Published simultaneously in Canada by
The Macmillan Company of Canada Limited

SBN 670–34777–9

Library of Congress catalog card number: 74–7507

Color photographs printed in Japan

Text printed in U.S.A.

CONTENTS

ACKNOWLEDGMENTS

My special gratitude goes to Nicolas Ducrot, whose enthusiasm started this project, and to Mary Velthoven, who carried it on as my editor. For most photographers, editing their own pictures is painful, and I especially want to thank Bryan Holme, who made the final picture selection process not only less painful but downright exciting.

There were many Park Service people who offered time and help to me willingly; so many, in fact, that it is difficult to list them all, but thanks are in order, at least, to Tony Bevinetto at Grand Teton National Park and to my old friend Paul Fritz, Superintendent of the Craters of the Moon National Monument, who gave me frequent advice and help.

Finally, over the years when this project was under way I received much encouragement and help from a family that is lucky enough to have the Grand Tetons in its front yard. I am indebted to Mrs. Margaret Murie and to Adolph and Louise Murie for all their kindness and help.

INTRODUCTION

Headed west in 1960, fresh from college with a degree in physics and an eye toward California, land of sunshine and aerospace industry, I took a wrong turn in the middle of Wyoming, or thought I did at the time. I wanted to see Yellowstone, make one of those typical in-and-out-of-the-park trips, mostly to confirm the wild stories I'd read about the place. My road map had been lost for days, buried somewhere in a backseat that was full of clothes and empty beer cans, but I knew where I was going and I knew that somewhere just before Yellowstone I would pass a mountain range called the Tetons. That name conjured up dim memories, from an old calendar photograph, perhaps, or a travel article, of towering peaks covered with a frosting of dazzling snow.

West of Riverton and across hot, shimmering desert, the blue forms of mountains took shape. By Dubois they were confirmed, rough, rugged mountains jutting out of a deep-green sea of forest —the Tetons, obviously. (Actually, as I was to learn later, what I was seeing was part of the southern Absaroka Range.) The highway continued on, climbing upward and apparently *through* the range. Funny. I didn't recall the map showing any highway cutting across the Tetons. Near the top of Togwotee Pass I stopped to breathe in that crisp air, take a picture of the great cliffs towering above, and listen to a Californian brag to another tourist about why he lived in the land of smog instead of here: "Ya can't eat scenery." ("Fortunately," I added to myself.)

I was totally unprepared for what happened next. Having seen and crossed the "Tetons," I continued my journey. In a few miles I rounded a bend on the west side of Togwotee Pass and very nearly drove off the road. Before me was the most stunning panorama I had ever seen. Laid out like a lush green carpet below me was the valley of Jackson Hole. And at the far edge of that carpet, poking upward like carnivorous teeth into a deep-blue Wyoming sky, were the most incredible mountains. No. They couldn't be real. They must be the leftover backdrop from some Hollywood extravaganza. Even in my wildest dreams I couldn't have conceived a range of peaks so awful, so bristling, so wild and rugged and magnificent. But there they were. As I drove closer the first impressions were amplified. They *were* awful, looming like spiked giants over Jackson Hole. Frightening. And fascinating.

I never made it to California or the aerospace industry, choosing instead to settle somewhere near these magnificent Tetons—*my* Tetons. (I secretly laid claim to them that day on Togwotee Pass.) And thus began what was to become—and remain—a love affair with a mountain range.

Somewhere, somehow, sometime all of us stake out a mental claim to a piece of earth, a particular geography, or a certain land form. It's a sense of being at home with the land, feeling comfortable and comforted by those special surroundings. There are desert rats who thrive in a sun-seared land of cactus and slickrock. I'm a part-time desert rat myself. Some people cannot live without the pounding, moody ocean nearby. For others (call them flatlanders, if you will), it's the level grasslands of the high plains where you can see day-after-tomorrow's weather coming on. And then there are us mountain folk. Or freaks. Or maniacs. We love the biting cold and deep snows of winter. We live for those brief alpine summers of green meadows and splashy wild flowers, sun-warmed rock and treeless tundra, slashing storms and dancing, teeth-aching, cold, cold streams. We do crazy things like strap on a heavy pack and hike a dozen, grueling uphill miles to sit by a little alpine lake all alone, and maybe get rained, hailed, or snowed on in the process. Or we scare the bejezus out of ourselves by climbing to the tops of some of those mountains we love.

To be more specific, however, there are certain places within each of those land forms where one really feels a close tie to the land—a feeling of belonging, I guess. The desert rat may love all deserts, but if he were to choose the one place in which to live—or die—it might be, say, Escalante or Cabeza Prieta. And for certain mountain folk it may be the San Juans, the Cascades, the Sawtooths, the Sierras, the Uintahs, the Wind River range or Big Horn Mountains. For me it's the Teton country. Why? Who knows?

I've often sworn to people (no one believes me) that I could be transported—blindfolded—from any place on earth and set down in this Jackson Hole–Teton–Yellowstone country (away from any obvious landmarks, of course) and I could tell instantly that I was home. I could tell by the forests: by the slim and spare lodgepoles that reach upward with delicate grace; by the aspen, where the wind plays gentle music through the leaves; and, of course, by the perfect spires of alpine fir. I could probably tell from just the smells alone: the pungent and sensuous aroma of sagebrush, the resinous perfume of coniferous forests, and the crisp cleanness of pure air, unsoiled, unspoiled. And, if all else failed, the flowers alone might do it. Is there anywhere else on earth where paintbrush is so brilliant, so psychedelic a red?

I suppose my senses are aided by something mystical, something I can't quite explain. It's the *feeling* of this country, a combination of sights and sounds and smells and something extrasensory. I feel that I belong here. This is *my* country.

In the beginning, I didn't feel this way about the Teton country. Used to the riotous, tangled growth of eastern forests that cloaks everything from valley to mountaintop, I wasn't prepared for the austerity, the sparseness of undergrowth in the forest, or the nakedness of bare rock above timberline. Even though I was awed by the magnificent splendor of the Tetons, I was also a little over-

10

whelmed by them. The first explorations began timidly.

Many of my Teton trips have been fiascos. I seem to have the knack for being in the right place at the wrong time and for being ill prepared for unknown terrain. Nonetheless, the trips have been memorable and enjoyable. There was that one occasion when Tom Davis, Pat Mahoney, and I attempted a trip across the range via Darby Canyon, and were stopped short by an eight-hundred-foot cliff that didn't show on a map with two-hundred-foot contour intervals, and then there was that all night rain in Alaska Basin with five of us sharing a few square feet of plastic tarp for shelter (it didn't shelter). And there was that conversation that took place on a dark February night on a ski-touring trip to Taggart Lake:

> Scratch, scratch, scratch.
> "Jerry."
> Silence.
> "Jerry!"
> "Hmph."
> "Wake up; there's something into your pack."
> "Huh?"
> Fumble about in the blackness of the tent for flashlight and glasses.
> Scratch, scratch.
> "Hear him?"
> "Yeah. Wonder what it is."
> "Bear?"
> "No, not this time of year."
> "Where's that damn flashlight? There, I found it."
> Cold fingers fumble at the tent zipper.
> "There he is."
> "Where? Hell, my glasses are fogged."
> Two glowing eyes stare back.
> "What is it? Looks like a mink."
> "I think it's a marten."
> Golden fur flows over the snow, then pauses to sit up and glare at the intruders who interrupted his forage.
> "Pretty, isn't he?"
> "You wouldn't say that if it was your pack he was into."
> "You need to lose a little weight anyway. Hey, I thought martens turned white in winter."
> Silence.
> "Jerry?"
> "Hmmph?"
> "Never mind."
> Scratch, scratch.

A marten. On other occasions, a bear. Stumbling tiredly down a trail, turning a corner, and coming eyeball to eyeball with a big bull moose—it's all a part of the country, the experience. So, too, is sitting under an overhang in Cascade Canyon watching hour after hour of steady rain while munching raisins and a soggy peanut butter sandwich and discussing worldly things, or wondering if your feet and legs will hold up coming down that terrible moraine of the Teton Glacier. The miseries. Or were they?

And the joys: discovering some alpine lakes high in the Western Slopes that weren't on any maps; discovering, in fact, that there *weren't* any maps of this country. (There are now, unfortunately.) Standing in the precise spot where William H. Jackson made the first photographs of the Tetons more than a century ago and finding it virtually unchanged, or taking that exhausting and exhilarating last step onto a high summit and looking down at the world from a lofty height of bare granite and purple sky—these are moments that add up to a strong sense of place.

One learns best about a land by walking through it, climbing its peaks, wading its streams, sleeping in its folds, getting rained or snowed on, being exposed to the good and the bad, the pleasant and the frightening, the enjoyable and the miserable, feeling tired, excited, relaxed, elated, sad, being cold, hot, wet, or parched. One learns to love a land that offers all these things. The Tetons have been generous, but not all the discoveries have been pleasant. Slowly one comes to the realization that, with precious little wilderness left, some people are out to conquer it all, turn lovely forests into dollars, gouge mountains for minerals of dubious value, pave everything in sight. I remember sitting one afternoon in an alpine meadow above North Leigh Canyon in the Western Slopes with Al McGlinsky, Jerry Jayne, and Jim Campbell. This forgotten side of the Tetons, comprising about half of the range, is without benefit of national park protection. Pleasantly tired, we were resting on the return leg of a weekend backpacking trip. Suddenly, far off in the forest below us, came the high-pitched whine of a chain saw. Miles away, it pierced the high thin air, shattering peace and tranquility. Worse than the immediate intrusion of noise, however, was the ominous prophecy of things to come. Was this lovely area also to be sacrificed on the altar of false progress? As I sat there I felt a tightening knot in the pit of my stomach, a knot of fear and rage and panic. Anger later led to action. A number of us prepared a proposal for the U.S. Forest Service asking for the preservation of these Western Slopes as a Wilderness Area. I am cautiously optimistic that the region will be saved, either by establishment of a Wilderness Area or by adding it to Grand Teton National Park as it should have been years ago.

This action on my part was the start of a deepening involvement in conservation, an involvement that was to change my life. I suppose you could say that the Tetons were responsible for it all—for the discovery of wilderness, of natural beauty unrivaled, of adventure and even danger, for an encounter with myself and with a different set of values and another way of life. The Tetons have had a profound effect on me. I suppose they've been affecting people in similar ways for more than a century, perhaps even for the thousands of years that men have lived near them.

This book, then, is the personal record of all these discoveries, though I must add a confession: I have not told all or pictured all here. Why? Because I'm selfishly hoarding a few secret places to myself. (Lord knows, it's hard enough to do in these times when everyone seems to be strapping on a backpack to escape from the madness we've created.) And so, stashed away in these mountains are a few little jewels that I try to visit from time to time, places for which I've come to have a strong feeling of stewardship. I take care of them and they, in turn, provide me with many pleasures.

Thus I end my introduction with a plea, not only for my own special places, but for all the secret places in the Tetons: tread lightly, for these are the only Tetons we will ever have.

CREATION

In the making of mountains, as in all else, Nature is an unsparing self-critic, never satisfied, never considering her task finished. Could human life flow on as continuously as do the mountain streams, we should discover that the Teton peaks and canyons, in common with landscapes every-where, pass ceaselessly on from form to form.

—Fritiof Fryxell, *The Tetons: Interpretations of a Mountain Landscape*

The grass picked up the rhythm of the warm wind blowing unhindered across the land. Wave upon wave of swaying stalks rippled in concert across the prairie toward the low eastern hills where dark coniferous forests plunged into the grassy sea. Gnarled and stubbled sage dotted the undulating hills, while on drier, south-facing hillsides twisted junipers clawed at the unbroken blue sky.

The river, gathering waters from the volcanic uplands to the north, emptied into a broad, shallow lake where great flocks of birds congregated. In earlier times there had been giant mammals roaming this land, but several million years of violent volcanic activity had driven most of the beasts away. The outpouring of lava and rains of cinders had left the land sterile and lifeless. Only now, eons later, was it again fertile. And, in this era of relative quiet, a slow migration of some larger mammals brought occasional groups of antelope and small horses to graze upon the plentiful grasses. The brontotherium, largest of all land mammals that once roamed this area before the volcanoes, was now extinct; a victim, perhaps, of its own cumbersome size.

Suddenly, the slight breeze died and a strange and ominous quiet settled on the plain. Antelope froze, jerking their heads erect to scan for danger. Waterfowl on the lake fluttered nervously, ready to take flight in an instant.

It began as a low-pitched murmur, building quickly to a distant rumble not unlike thunder—

but there were no storms that day on the plain. Then the earth began to vibrate and new ripples spread out across the grass. The birds were first to panic and take flight, rising like a black cloud from the lake. The antelope and other grazing animals fled in wild panic, dashing madly in all directions trying to escape the shaking earth, as the rumble grew to a roar and the earth trembled violently. The once calm lake, now lashed with huge waves, seemed on the verge of being tipped and emptied by the shaking ground. In the low hills to the east and north huge trees toppled, striking others in their fall. Only the young and the supple seemed to survive. Everywhere, on the plain and in the forest, cracks had opened up in the soil.

It was over in a matter of minutes. But when quiet again came there was a new feature on the face of the land. Several miles west of the lake and river stood a small, freshly scarred ridge where none had been before. For forty miles or more it flowed across the plain in a north-south direction. In some places it was a few feet high, fresh rock draped with the still moist sod and grass it had ripped and parted in pushing its way up into the sunlight. In other places, where the faulted rock had not quite broken through the soil, the ridge was barely noticeable. It was not an imposing feature. Even if there had been a comprehending mind on hand to consider the matter, it is doubtful that this small disturbance of the earth would have been recognized as the start of a mountain range.

With the exception of many animal species which are no longer here, the scene could well be that of any typical western prairie today. The locale is, of course, western Wyoming. But the time is about nine million years ago.

In geological time there are no real beginnings and certainly no endings. All events are ultimately related to all others, and thus what was beginning on this peaceful plain had its real origins countless eons before.

Starting more than two billion years ago, a molten magma had welled up from deep in the earth, intruding into older, existing rocks. In cooling, this rich, superheated broth precipitated from its complex chemistry the feldspars, micas, quartz, hornblende, and dozens of other minerals to form the crystalline rock called granite.

Then, for several hundred million years there was mountain building; upthrusting and folding of the earth's crust. There may have been peaks greater than the Himalayas—there was time for that, and more—but no one will ever know, for time removed them all grain by grain.

For the next several hundred million years vast seas invaded the now flat and featureless land, seas that deposited on their murky bottoms the sediments that would later become shales, sandstones, and limestones. Intermittently the seas receded and the land rose into the sunlight. And then, for millions of years more, it was inundated again.

By thirty million years ago the last of the seas had receded and a new mountain building cycle was under way. Along a chain from Alaska to Mexico the restless crust of the earth folded and faulted in numerous places to produce the incipient Rocky Mountains. To the east and north of this pre-Teton plain, volcanoes spewed lava and cinders onto the land, shaping new features. And by about nine million years ago the volcanic plateau of Yellowstone was coming to life with eruptions that extruded molten lava southward across portions of the plain. The stage was thus set for the birth of the Tetons.

It may have been years, and perhaps centuries, between earthquakes which jarred the land. When they came the ridge moved upward again along a now-established path of weakness, exposing more and more rock. Perhaps there were days and weeks of nearly constant tremors, and then centuries of silence. Slowly the ridge grew, each new slippage adding to its height. The rocks that sheared and crumbled and rose above the flat land were sedimentaries, the shales and sandstones and limestones born during the generations of seas. Each new upthrust exposed older and older layers.

Neither the number nor the magnitudes of all these movements are known. But even throughout the relatively young life of the Tetons a seemingly slow rate of growth could produce impressive results. For example, if only once every five hundred years geological forces had added a mere foot of height to this range, then at the end of nine million years an incredible eighteen thousand feet of mountain wall would have towered over Jackson Hole, rather than the seven thousand feet we see today. Simple growth rates alone do not explain the shaping of mountains, for when this forty-mile wedge, abrupt on the east and sloping gently to the west, had risen high enough it began to bring about some slow and subtle changes. The warm, moist air that blew unhindered across the land was now forced upward to cooler elevations where it released its moisture as rain and snow. The force of gravity then drew the accumulated waters to gentler levels, first as trickles, then as torrents, and the scourings of these streams began to erode and shape the ridge. The sedimentaries, because of their relative softness, were carved easily into broad canyons. Little by little, the layers of rock were transported away by the streams and by the Snake River.

The range continued to grow, despite the forces working to tear it down. After a few million years the sedimentary layers, some three thousand feet thick, were raised high enough to expose the first glint of that crystallized magma which had remained hidden beneath them for eons. With time, this gleaming granite also moved slowly upward into the sunlight.

Sometime in its early life the mountain range developed complex shear zones. Instead of being thrust upward as one continuous wedge, the central region was pushed higher than the rest of the ridge by transverse faults. The increasing height steepened the gradient of the streams and speeded their cutting action. The erosion forces slowed somewhat when they had cut down through the softer sedimentaries and encountered the hard granite, but soon this too yielded, and sharply notched canyons were formed. In time, most of the sedimentary cap in the central portion of the range was eroded away, leaving the bare, gleaming granite. There may have been periods when violent quakes shook the land several times a century for many centuries, and the range grew higher; then the range may have sat placidly for longer periods while erosion slowly wore it away. The force that raised these mountains was large but intermittent. The counterforce that sought to tear it down was small but continuous. Together, they worked to shape the rough-cut forms of the Teton Range. The final faceting was done by ice.

The ice of the ice ages began as snow. About a quarter of a million years ago in North America the first of three climatic changes began which resulted in extensive glaciation. The reasons for these climatic changes aren't clearly understood, but perhaps alterations of ocean currents, variations in solar energy and carbon dioxide in the atmosphere, or other factors produced a period of lengthening winters. During these times the summer sun no longer melted all of winter's snow and gradually an excess accumulated in the higher mountain canyons and among the peaks. Compressed under its own ever-increasing weight, the snow was transformed into ice. In time, the steep canyons of the Teton Range were nearly filled with frozen rivers which spilled out into Jackson Hole to join larger glacial fields fanning out from ranges to the north and east. With powerful effect, the ice fields chipped, scoured, and scraped away at the hard granite. The V-shaped canyons were broadened. But more importantly, perhaps, the great peaks of the range—Grand Teton, Mount Owen, Mount Tee-winot, Middle and South Tetons, and others—were sharpened and faceted into the jagged forms we see today.

This first and most extensive of the glacial epochs gave way to warmer times and the ice fields gradually disappeared, leaving the land cloaked with boulders and morainal debris. Slowly the land recovered, regained its soil. Grass and forest once again grew in the valley and crept upward into the mountains.

The next glaciation occurred between thirty-five and eighty thousand years ago. Though not as extensive as the first, the rivers of ice once again marched down the canyons to join an ice field in Jackson Hole. Then, with warmer times, this period also passed.

The third and latest glacial epoch began roughly twelve thousand to fifteen thousand years ago. It was less extensive than the earlier ones. Nonetheless, all the major canyons of the range, from Death Canyon to Moran Canyon, held large glaciers that moved slowly out into the valley. Evidence indicates that these last glaciers remained until at least nine thousand years ago, into the time when man inhabited this region. In the lava desert country west of the range, in Idaho's Snake River plain, there are caves, within sight of the Tetons, that show evidence of man's habitation as far back as twelve thousand years ago. As the glaciers slowly receded, they left a string of jewel-like lakes at the base of the mountains. Gradually, vegetation replaced the glaciers, first with tundra grasses and later with forests.

Today all of these geological forces are still at work. Tremors indicate that the range is still growing, though there hasn't been a major and violent upthrust during the miniscule amount of time that man has been measuring it all. The elements still continue, inexorably, to tear the range down, grain by grain. And tucked away in the shady recesses of high cirques and basins are the remnants of those once-mighty glaciers, biding time until the cycle turns and they may crawl forth once again to rule the land.

16

EXPLORATION

It is the time of fulfillment, the fullness of time, the moment lived for itself alone. The mountain men were a tough race, as many selective breeds of Americans have had to be; their courage, skill, and mastery of the conditions of their chosen life were absolute or they would not have been here. Nor would they have been here if they had not responded to the loveliness of the country and found in their way of life something precious beyond safety, gain, comfort, and family life.

—Bernard De Voto, *Across the Wide Missouri*

When President Thomas Jefferson consummated the purchase of the Louisiana Territory in 1803, he wasted no time in finding out what he had bought. Only days after the purchase he commissioned Captain Meriwether Lewis and Lieutenant William Clark to outfit an expedition "to explore the Missouri River, & such principal stream of it, as, by its course & communication with the waters of the Pacific Ocean, may offer the most direct & practicable water communication across this continent, for the purposes of commerce."

Although the Lewis and Clark expedition ultimately passed well north of it, this trip played a key role in the discovery and exploration of the Yellowstone and Teton region. It charted the unknown territory of the northern Rocky Mountains and paved the way for other explorers. And, although the expedition did not find that elusive Northwest Passage for easy navigation across the continent, it did reinforce the United States' claim to the Oregon Territory which, "for the purposes of commerce," marked the beginning of commercial ventures into both the Northwest and the Rocky Mountain region. The man who discovered Yellowstone and the Teton Range was a member of that expedition. His name was John Colter.

Colter was a bold adventurer and something of an enigma in the history of the West. He signed up to join Lewis and Clark in October of 1803 and stayed with the group through the hardships of traversing the rugged northern Rockies, traveling to the Pacific shore, and returning over nearly the same route in 1806. A journey of this nature would seem adventure enough for any man, and yet, before the party returned to civilization, Colter asked for and received permission to leave the group in order to join two trappers bound for the upper reaches of the Yellowstone River.

The Lewis and Clark expedition returned without him, and Colter, with his two companions, departed for the unknown upper Yellowstone in August of 1806. Unfortunately there is no record of this trio's wanderings. Colter mysteriously appeared alone in the spring of 1807 in time to join the Missouri Fur Company near the confluence of the Platte and the Missouri Rivers. Then, once again, he set out for the upper Yellowstone.

This time, however, there is ample evidence concerning the extent and nature of his journey. He apparently passed to the east of present-day Yellowstone National Park and headed south until he reached the Wind River. Following this river to its source, he crossed Union Pass and entered Jackson Hole from the southeast in the summer or fall of 1807. After exploring the lovely valley of Jackson Hole below the magnificent Teton Range, he crossed Teton Pass and entered Pierre's Hole in what is now Teton Valley, Idaho. He spent the winter of 1807–1808 at the base of the Western Slopes of the Tetons. Continuing his journey in the spring, he probably crossed the gentler northern Tetons, entering the Yellowstone country on his return trip. In a report, Clark made note of Colter's journey and assigned to him the discovery of two large bodies of water known today as Yellowstone and Jackson Lakes. No mention was made, however, of the range of mountains to become known as the Tetons.

Only two years later colleagues of Colter's from the Missouri Fur Company were forced to flee their fort, located northwest of Yellowstone, because of Indian attacks. They headed south over the Continental Divide to the North Fork of the Snake River where they built a fort near the present-day town of St. Anthony, Idaho, a short distance from the western Tetons. These mountain men, led by Andrew Henry, wintered here and trapped the Teton country, crossing over into Jackson Hole on occasion. In the spring the trappers left. The main group, under Henry, returned down the Missouri, retracing their route. But three of them, John Hoback, John Robinson, and Jacob Reznor, chose to head east over Teton Pass, across Jackson Hole, then over Togwotee Pass before trekking overland to the Missouri River.

The next journey into the region was another commercial venture. John Jacob Astor, seeking to expand his fur-trading empire, funded an expedition to follow the track of Lewis and Clark from Missouri to the mouth of the Columbia, there to establish a fort to serve as a center of commerce and exploitation of the Northwest. Wilson Price Hunt was the leader of this party. Another Astor group left by ship to sail around Cape Horn to the Columbia, and it was planned that this second party, after meeting with Hunt, would retrace the overland route back to Missouri.

Hunt began his trip in 1811 by following Lewis and Clark's route up the Missouri River, but he soon departed from it when a report arrived of hostile Indians ahead. The report was delivered by Hoback, Reznor, and Robinson, who met Hunt on the Missouri while on their return trip from the Teton country. Signing the trio on as hunters and scouts, Hunt then proceeded overland along the route the three men had taken. Ascending the Wind River as Colter had four years before, they arrived in the vicinity of Union Pass where, according to the account in Washington Irving's *Astoria:* "In the course of the day, they came to a height that commanded an almost boundless prospect. Here one of the guides paused, and, after considering the vast landscape attentively, pointed to three mountain peaks glistening with snow, which rose, he said, above a fork of the Columbia River. They were hailed by the travellers with that joy which a beacon on a seashore is hailed by mariners after a long and dangerous voyage."

The peaks were, of course, the Tetons. But, according to Irving, it was not to be Hunt who would name them such; "as guiding points for many days, to Mr. Hunt, he gave them the names of the Pilot Knobs."

The unimaginative Mr. Hunt moved on, following the river named for John Hoback to the confluence of the Snake—which he dubbed the Mad River—then over Teton Pass and across Pierre's Hole to the site of Fort Henry. After much hardship, the Hunt expedition was successful, arriving at the mouth of the Columbia River to meet the seagoing party.

In the early summer of 1812 the return party, headed by Robert Stuart, left the fort at Astoria on the Columbia and retraced Hunt's route. As they neared the area of Jackson Hole, Indian attacks and sickness caused them to retrace their path a short distance down the Snake River and head up the North Fork toward Pierre's Hole. Still besieged by sickness and the threat of further Indian attacks, Stuart wrote in his journal, while camped in the shadow of the Tetons, "The sensations excited on this occasion and by the view of an unknown & untravelled wilderness are not such as arise in the artificial solitude of parks and gardens, for there one is apt to indulge a flattering notion of self sufficiency, as well as a placid indulgence of voluntary delusions; whereas the phantoms which haunt a desert are want, misery, and danger, the evils of dereliction rush upon the mind; man is made unwillingly acquainted with his own weakness, and meditation shows him only how little he can sustain and how little he can perform . . ."

Despite their low spirits, the Stuart party moved on, over Teton Pass and up the Hoback Canyon, ultimately returning to St. Louis in the spring of 1813.

The Teton country now basked again in relative solitude, visited only by those native people who lived nearby, hunting and fishing the lands and the streams of the Teton country as their ancestors had for twelve thousand years or more. To the Indians, those first, brief invasions of their domain by white men must have had ominous overtones.

The next group of trappers came from the west, and they were British, members of a company that was soon to become a part of the famous Hudson's Bay Company. In 1818 or 1819 a party headed by Donald McKenzie explored the Teton and Yellowstone country. Since they approached from the west, their first glimpse of the range was of three pointed peaks, which prompted some French–Canadian trappers in the party to name them "Les Trois Tétons" (the three breasts). And one of those Frenchmen was to have a lovely valley—Pierre's Hole—named for him.

A whim of fashion was to mark the fate of the Teton country for the next twenty years. There were fortunes to be made in the lowly beaver whose pelt, fashioned into tall hats, was the rage of contemporary society in the East and in Europe. Companies were formed and expeditions funded to trap the bountiful streams and rivers of the upper Snake and Green River country. It all started in earnest in the early 1820s, the beginning of the "Golden Era" of the Mountain Men.

The men came by the hundreds, and they worked for such companies as the Rocky Mountain Fur Company, Hudson's Bay Company, and John Jacob Astor's American Fur Company. There were "free trappers" and small bands who operated without a formal company name. Some of the men themselves were to become legends in the history of the West: James Bridger, Jedediah Smith, the Sublette brothers, William and Milton, Joseph Meek, David Jackson, Thomas Fitzpatrick, Nathaniel Wyeth, Captain Benjamin L. E. Bonneville, Andrew Drips, Lucien Fontenelle, General William Ashley, Major Andrew Henry, and a host of others who were not to become so famous, but who would share the adventures of exploring the wild Rocky Mountain West.

Like gold, the fur trade provided quick fortunes for some. How quickly fortunes were made can be told by the turnover in ownership of the lucrative Rocky Mountain Fur Company. Founded in 1822 by General William Ashley and Major Andrew Henry, it was sold in 1826 to three of their ablest employees, Jed Smith, William Sublette, and Davey Jackson. In a brief four-year period Ashley and Henry had made their fortunes. Four years after that, Smith, Sublette, and Jackson sold out to Jim Bridger, Tom Fitzpatrick, Milton Sublette, and two others—all employees who had worked to amass a fortune for the three owners. None of the sets of owners were absentee directors, however. They worked hard themselves, leading parties of their employees into this wilderness country. They trapped, hunted, fought off Indian attacks, and braved the dangers of grizzly bears and treacherous rivers right along with their men. And, as Bernard De Voto so well pointed out, it was not solely profit which spurred them on. There was new country to be seen, lands that white men had never laid eyes on before.

Jed Smith was a particularly restless wanderer. He roamed far, making two trips to the Spanish settlements in California and poking around in much of the country in-between. The trappers ranged over much of the northern and central Rockies—farther, perhaps, than they really needed for beaver alone. There was, undoubtedly, a drive to see what was beyond that next mountain range. But they always returned to the Teton country, and here they had their favorite spots. The spectacular valley (valleys were often referred to as "holes" by the trappers) east of the Tetons held a special attraction for Davey Jackson, and eventually it was given his name: Jackson's Hole. For Jim Bridger, it was Pierre's Hole, which he called the "most beautiful valley in the world"—and he had seen a lot of them.

Unlike the gold seekers to come in a few decades, the mountain men had relatively little impact on the land. Rather than attempting to change it, as others would, they adapted. They learned much from the Indians and this knowledge enabled them to survive the harshness of the wilderness. Moreover, there seemed to be among them a profound feeling for beauty, wildness, and adventure.

With only a few exceptions, the mountain men built no permanent structures. For trading purposes they initiated the annual "rendezvous" system, a sort of wilderness trading mart where supplies from the East were brought in and beaver pelts were bartered and sold. The site of the annual rendezvous differed from year to year with many being held in the upper Green River area to the south of Jackson Hole. In 1832 the rendezvous was in Pierre's Hole. Like all others, it was a time of celebration and drinking as well as trading. It was said that there were frequently more casualties from the rendezvous than from the Indians. But bruised heads and monumental hangovers were to be taken in stride.

This era of the lusty, adventurous mountain men might have continued for decades but for two factors. First, their success as trappers was depleting the resource. Beavers were becoming scarce. Second, and most significant, the whims of fashion changed once more and the market for beaver pelts declined. By the early 1840s the fur trade was a dying industry and the trappers, undoubtedly with reluctance, were moving on. A few stayed around until the middle of the decade, but soon even the hangers-on were forced to depart. Once again the Teton country was left in relative solitude.

The discovery of gold farther west had little immediate impact on the Tetons. The trails that carried the hundreds of thousands of prospectors to California were well south of here, though a few men took the time to detour and see what riches might be found in the region. Fortunately, the Tetons held no mineral wealth. Had there been gold, the Tetons might have been scoured and scarred and torn apart in the search, for gold seekers are largely a greedy, insensitive lot and their impact on land is large and lasting. While the insane pursuit of gold swept over much of the West, the valleys of the Tetons remained quiet and unknown for almost twenty years.

Around 1860 a period of rediscovery began. Government funded expeditions were organized to explore the mythical region of the upper Yellowstone. Even though much of the West had been roamed and combed by this time, this particular area was still a land of mystery and legend. The tales of Bridger and his colleagues about smoking mountains and boiling springs in Yellowstone had been scoffed at. And yet, stories of such features continued to trickle out of the region for decades, providing excitement enough to spur further exploration.

First came the Raynold expedition of 1860, with Jim Bridger as guide. They traveled through Jackson and Pierre's Holes on their way to Yellowstone for the U.S. Topological Engineers. Ten years later came the Washburn–Doane expedition, significant *not* for its exploration of the Tetons (the party largely confined its wanderings to Yellowstone) but for an idea spawned by them: the creation of a National Park. Two years later the new concept would be realized with the establishment by Congress of Yellowstone National Park. Curiously, the Teton Range—long considered a part of the general Yellowstone country—was not included in the park. It would be more than fifty years before the Tetons were afforded protection.

Beginning in 1871, and continuing for nearly a decade, there were expeditions into the mountains under the leadership of Dr. Ferdinand V. Hayden, Director of the U.S. Geological Survey. These early Hayden expeditions were important not only for their thoroughness, but for the pictorial records made by the famous photographer William Henry Jackson and the equally renowned artist Thomas Moran. Jackson and Moran captured on film and canvas the beauty of Yellowstone and the Tetons. Jackson roamed over a significant part of the Teton Range, in particular the Western Slopes where he made the first photographs of Grand Teton and other peaks.

In 1872 two members of the Hayden expedition, Nathaniel P. Langford and James Stevenson, made the first apparent recorded ascent of Grand Teton. (There is still considerable controversy as to whether this party actually reached the summit or not.) Their approach began from the Western Slopes, following the South Fork of Teton Creek up into Alaska Basin where they set up camp. Crossing over the drainage divide into the South Fork of Cascade Canyon, they made their way past Icefloe Lake and up to the Lower Saddle, the connecting ridge between Grand and Middle Tetons. Scrambling upward from there they encountered the difficult west flank of Grand Teton. After what Langford described as "ten hours of the severest labor of my life," they reached the summit— 13,766 feet high.

The romantic era of exploration of the Teton country drew to a close with the ending of the Hayden expeditions. The photographs of Jackson, the paintings of Moran, and the words of Hayden and Langford and others revealed the secret of the Tetons to the nation. Soon the first tourists visited Yellowstone and settlers moved into the lovely valleys surrounding the Teton Range. Wild prairie grasses which fed the herds of bison and antelope were plowed under for crops or were relegated to cattle and sheep. The grizzly bear, menace to cattle and sometimes to man, was hunted and driven into its last sanctuary—Yellowstone. That most marked characteristic of civilization—the political boundary—divided and subdivided the land by imaginary and meaningless lines. The land itself, which Indians believed belonged to no one and offered sustenance to everyone, was claimed and settled and bartered and sold. Too soon the land was tamed, except for two islands of wilderness which still remain—Yellowstone and the Teton Range.

But saving the Tetons was not easy.

RECREATION

. . . its sharp, deep cañons, with massive, precipitous walls; its rugged, lofty peaks, together form a combination of beauty and grandeur rarely equaled. Though its peaks are surpassed by many in actual elevation above the sea, few such stand among so broad, deep valleys as to give so great relative elevations and to be seen so prominently over so wide an extent of country. When the region becomes more accessible by means of already projected railroads, this must become a favorite resort for tourists.

—Frank H. Bradley, Hayden Survey of 1872

In the years that followed the establishment of Yellowstone National Park in 1872, there were some recurring questions: Why hadn't the Tetons been made a part of Yellowstone National Park? (Most of the early trappers and explorers considered Jackson Hole, the Teton Range and Pierre's Hole on the west all a part of the general "Yellowstone Country.") What was to be the fate of the magnificent Teton Range and Jackson Hole? Should the valley and these mountains be preserved as a separate park?

In an attempt to halt destruction by the reckless timber barons of the West, President Theodore Roosevelt established a system of Forest Preserves under control of the Federal Government, a system that was the forerunner of the National Forests. The Tetons became a part of the Teton Forest Preserve, established in 1897, but the protection afforded was minimal. Mining was still allowed and no guarantee was granted against other commercial development. And the valley, of course, had no protection at all.

As settlers moved into the region, most of Jackson Hole was carved into ranches and there was little immediate concern about preservation of the scenery. In time, however, some residents began to worry over signs of callous development and the threat of irrigation schemes that would use the lovely lakes at the base of the range. Fearing that the beauty of the region would be marred, a small group of Jackson Hole residents met in 1923 with Horace Albright, then Superintendent of Yellowstone, to discuss means of preserving a portion of the region. There was no immediate action, but the seeds of a plan were sown and soon began growing.

John D. Rockefeller, Jr., who owned the JY Ranch near Phelps Lake, began to take an interest in the preservation of the area. In 1926 he established the Snake River Land Company to begin quietly purchasing private lands in Jackson Hole. His plan was to turn over these lands to the Federal Government for preservation. In the meantime, support for a park continued to grow and in 1929 President Calvin Coolidge signed into law the bill establishing Grand Teton National Park. The new park consisted of the rugged Teton Range plus a small fringe of valley lands immediately adjacent to the mountains, a total of ninety-six thousand acres—less than a third of today's park area. It was Rockefeller's plan to continue to acquire many of the valley ranch lands to add to the park. But during the next two decades bitterness developed over the expansion of Grand Teton National Park.

Where initially there had been support for preserving the area, now there was growing opposition. Cattlemen feared that further Federal encroachment would limit or perhaps curtail grazing rights. The citizens were led to believe that removal of private lands from the tax rolls would bankrupt the county. The 1930s and 1940s became a stormy period for the park. Several bills were introduced in Congress to expand the park to include more of Jackson Hole. As opposition mounted, all these measures failed to pass. Finally, in 1943 President Franklin Roosevelt felt compelled to move lest the opportunity of acquiring the Rockefeller lands be lost. Acting under the Antiquities Act of 1906, he signed a Presidential Proclamation establishing the Jackson Hole National Monument comprised of the Rockefeller purchases plus federal lands in the northern and eastern portion of the valley.

This move seemed to confirm local suspicions of government takeover and precipitated swift action on the part of Wyoming lawmakers. Bills to abolish Jackson Hole National Monument were introduced almost immediately and some came perilously close to passage. On one occasion, only the President's threat of a veto prevented congressional action. For some residents of the valley fighting against preservation of any of Jackson Hole became a tireless campaign. Even as late as 1947 Congress held public hearings on a bill to abolish the Monument.

Throughout this era of discord a small but solid core of citizens continued to support the preservation of the Tetons and Jackson Hole. Eventually their devotion was rewarded. In 1950 a bill was signed into law establishing a new Grand Teton National Park which included nearly all of the lands of Jackson Hole National Monument plus the previous park lands—310,000 acres in all in one unified park. Permanent protection for the region was thus assured. The beauty would be preserved for future generations. Or would it?

A visitor to Grand Teton National Park today may notice several important things. The lovely valley of Jackson Hole is still largely uncluttered; the works of man here are minimal. There is a sense of openness and freedom about this place, which undoubtedly would not have been maintained without the protection afforded by National Park status. The mountains, of course, have retained their grandeur and are every bit as inspiring to modern-day tourists as they were to the first explorers. They dominate the landscape; everywhere one goes in the park these peaks loom above. And even in storms, when they are shrouded with a heavy mantle of clouds, one senses their presence.

But somehow the scene is not as peaceful and sublime as one would like. Something disturbs. There's a sense of gathering trouble in this Shangri-la, an uneasiness that may boil over into frustration and anger on a hot day when traffic is jammed bumper to bumper on park roads, or when every campground is filled to overflowing. Under these conditions people become livid with rage.

"Two thousand miles!" a man from Ohio says. Two thousand miles he has driven for a two-week vacation. And now the Park Ranger tells him there is no room in the campground. They stand beside his motor home. Obviously he has a right to be angry. He has been lied to. Led to believe that his motor home was the transport to idyllic tranquility, he is bitter upon discovering thousands of other people sharing the same notion and also the same campground. He has also been deceived by the Chamber of Commerce promotion that enticed him and others to come to Grand Teton National Park for a touch of wilderness beauty. No one mentions in those tourist brochures the three million people who flock here each summer for solitude and find none.

The Ranger is patient, obviously experienced at handling angry visitors. He quietly points out that there are only so many campgrounds in the park and only so many campsites in each one. They are all filled.

"Then it's up to you people to build more campgrounds," the man from Ohio erupts. Again with infinite patience the Ranger tries to explain that continued development of the park is self-defeating, that more roads and highways and campgrounds would consume the very natural beauty that people seek here. The man from Ohio is unconvinced as he storms away.

Unfortunately such encounters are no longer rare nor are they confined solely to the developed portions of the park. Backpackers and climbers are discovering that the wilderness also is becoming crowded. For years the detractors of the preservation philosophy of parks and wilderness areas have argued that only a "wealthy few" ever venture into wilderness country. But, as one Park Ranger points out, "There must be a hell of a lot of wealthy people in this country." In Grand Teton National Park the standard joke is that Lake Solitude (a moderately difficult trek of about nine miles into the heart of the range) should be renamed Lake Multitude. The problem grows more acute every year.

In recent years there has been much publicity concerning the problems of our National Parks; the problems of Grand Teton and nearby Yellowstone seem typical of some of the worst of these. While a great diversity of pressures plague our parks, most problems stem from the internal combustion engine. The very dependence of our culture on the automobile, coupled with increased leisure time, has brought increasing numbers of visitors flocking to our parks. One might also argue that more indirect forces such as urban blight and pollution provide impetus for people to escape. But what solutions are there to overuse and crowding in our National Parks?

In attempting to find an answer, it is probably best to begin by defining the National Park concept, or, more specifically, to ask what is Grand Teton National Park? What is the intent of this boundary drawn around some 310,000 acres?

Establishing the boundaries of Yellowstone was easy. A simple rectangle, generous in size was possible, because there were no competing uses for the land at that time. When Grand Teton was established, especially the "new" park, compromises were necessary: here a jog in the boundary to avoid a conflict, there another jog to include those hard-won Rockefeller lands. The result is a strangely irregular piece of land nearly touching Yellowstone on the north, tracing a zigzag pattern on the eastern edge of Jackson Hole, almost reaching the town of Jackson on the south, and following the drainage divide on the west. Nearly half of the Teton Range—the Western Slopes—is left out. But with all of its faults and compromises, within the protective boundary there is a natural community that includes the sagebrush flats of Jackson Hole, the river-bottom lands and marshes along the Snake River, the forested slopes and canyons, the alpine tundra, and the rugged expanse of snow and granite. It is a fascinating continuum of life and land forms still relatively unspoiled, an ecological wholeness that is both independent of man and at his mercy. Grand Teton National Park is a diverse and beautiful environment, enclosed by an imaginary and rather arbitrary line drawn in an attempt to hold back the sometimes subtle and often profane changes brought about by man and to preserve those physical entities whose values we seek to protect from the more destructive forces of our culture. But that protection is weakened continually, for even within those boundaries are avenues through which our culture has an adverse impact on some of those entities. Roads, highways, campgrounds, and other developments, many of which were products of a period of over-zealous development by the National Park Service, mar the park.

In recent years the National Park Service has taken serious steps toward solving some of the problems, and one of the most powerful tools to effect solutions was provided by the Wilderness Act of 1964. As stipulated by that act, the Service has conducted a ten-year review of the National Park System and will recommend some parks or portions of parks as candidates for protection in the Wilderness System. For Grand Teton some 116,000 acres, or about thirty-seven per cent of the park, has been proposed for wilderness protection, thus ensuring that at least that much of the park will remain free of developments.

Wilderness designation solves only a part of the problem. Urgently needed are means of regulating the increasing numbers who visit the park by automobile or who use the wilderness. The motorist and the backpacker represent two opposite and frequently conflicting viewpoints. The impact of the auto has been recognized for a long time, but only recently have we become aware that wilderness users are beginning to have an impact as well.

There has been a widespread assumption that virtually everyplace in the nation ought to be accessible by car. The effect of this emphasis is made more dramatic when we discover that this nation has paved significantly more land area in roads and highways than we've preserved in our total National Park System. Approximately 30 million acres are currently in the National Park System; an estimated 35 million acres are in use as paved roads, streets, highways, and parking lots. This disparity becomes greater each year as more and more land is dedicated to the auto while the National Park System rarely increases in size.

In order to cope with the growing problem of the automobile, the Park Service has in places initiated the use of mass transit systems with some degree of success. Plans are being developed for bus systems in Grand Teton National Park, but the perennially underfunded Park Service may have to wait before implementing such plans.

A reservation system for the use of campgrounds in Grand Teton has met with moderate success, but lack of widespread publicity has handicapped the program. To a large degree the success of all such schemes lies in the ability to reach and educate the public on the use of our National Parks. As one Park Service official points out, the time to begin dealing with the park visitor is before he even leaves home. The man from Ohio, had he been adequately warned of the prevailing crowded conditions in Grand Teton, might have chosen a different vacation locale. Perhaps he could have reserved a campsite in advance, or come prepared with backpacks for a trek into country where he could escape the frustrating crowds.

But what of the wilderness itself? Should dispersal of people from the developed portions of the park into the undeveloped parts be encouraged? Obviously, the wilderness, too, has a finite carrying capacity. In fact, the high-country wilderness, due to its more fragile nature, has a much smaller carrying capacity than valley lands and thus requires more stringent regulation of use. In Grand Teton National Park, as in a growing number of other parks, it is now necessary to reserve a back-country campsite. If a particular place is at carrying capacity, visitors are encouraged to change their backpacking itinerary and choose another campsite or destination. The general acceptance of such restrictions depends on a number of things. Some backpackers, for example, feel that these restrictions are illogical when the Park Service allows continued use of horses in the wilderness. Horse trips, long traditional in the West and in Grand Teton National Park, obviously have more impact on fragile wilderness than hikers and backpackers. Thus, it would seem imperative that the Park Service ultimately phase out the use of horses in park wilderness.

In recent years one important problem concerning Grand Teton National Park has been the Jackson Hole airport. Grand Teton is the only National Park containing an airport, or a portion of one, and at present there is limited commercial airline service via relatively quiet propjet planes. Commercial interests in the region are pushing for expansion of the facilities to accommodate large jets, and the prospect of a jetport inside a National Park is not pleasant. Conservationists argue that the high noise levels would constitute an intolerable intrusion and degrade the park experience. Superficially, at least, it would seem that air transport could be a mass transit alternative to auto travel. However, less than one per cent of all Grand Teton National Park visitors arrive by air and projections for expanded airline service indicate that this total may never exceed a few per cent.

It is easy to be misled in seeking solutions to the Teton jetport controversy. For example, an alternative jetport location has been suggested for Driggs, Idaho, in Teton Valley on the western side of the Teton Range. This would remove the airport from the park, but it would destroy another, relatively unspoiled part of the Teton country. The noise intrusion here would affect the area on the Western Slopes of the Tetons, proposed for reservation as wilderness or as an addition to Grand Teton National Park. No matter where it was located, the jetport would not contribute to solving transportation problems in the park itself. More basic is the failure once again to recognize the meaning and value of our National Parks as sanctuaries and natural museums which safeguard our increasingly rare wilderness and wildlife.

Such questions become increasingly important as places like Grand Teton National Park begin to have large economic impact on surrounding communities. Economic interests have been able to influence development and land-management decisions in the past, even within the National Parks, and such influence has rarely been of long-term benefit to the parks.

Economic pressure on the parks takes many forms. The Ashton-Flagg Ranch Road, a primitive but passable route, traverses the Teton Corridor, the narrow strip of land separating Yellowstone and Grand Teton National Parks. From Flagg Ranch near the south entrance of Yellowstone to Ashton, Idaho, this road bisects the heart of the transitional zone between the rugged Teton Range and the plateau area of Yellowstone. Ecologists feel that this is a biologically important area. It lies in the path of part of the seasonal elk migration and contains the headwaters of numerous lovely streams and rivers. For years motel and tourist interests have pushed hard to have this delightful, winding, old road turned into a modern high-speed highway, with massive recreation developments along its route. Conservationists have fought this proposal, but it seems clear that the battle may be won only by adding the Teton Corridor to either of the parks.

Equally endangered are the Western Slopes of the Tetons, a region lying west of the main peaks and containing some 200,000 acres of pristine forests, lakes, and mountains. This lovely and nearly forgotten wilderness, once known well by the mountain men, was roamed by the pioneer photographer William H. Jackson and artist Thomas Moran, and praised by Owen Wister in his novel *The Virginian*. The U.S. Forest Service, in whose jurisdiction this land currently falls, is completing a study of the suitability of designating the region a Wilderness Area under the provisions of the Wilderness Act. Logging and mining interests and some chamber of commerce groups resist such protection. The area should remain open to development, they maintain. The only effective means of protecting the area may be to add it to Grand Teton National Park. Such a measure would place the whole Teton Range under the unified management of the Park Service, rather than fragmenting control between the Forest Service on the Western Slopes and the Park Service in the present park.

With such a stormy past and an increasingly troubled present, the future of the Teton country is in doubt. Nearly everyone recognizes that control of a burgeoning population is a necessary first step toward solving most environmental problems. Even with a stable population, National Parks and Wilderness Areas will continue to be plagued by the direct and indirect impact of man. If present consumption patterns continue unchanged, more lands, many of them potential park and wilderness preserves, must be sacrificed for the resources to feed our voracious appetites. There may even come a time, given sufficient pressures, when Grand Teton National Park may have its forests stripped and its mountains mined. Or the Tetons and Yellowstone could become small islands in a vast, smoky sea of civilization, a place where people would queue up, tickets in hand, to wait for a brief chance to sit under a tree or see an elk. By today's standards, such prospects are frightening.

But it is also possible that today's spark of environmental concern may be fanned into a blaze of environmental conscience. By altering our consumption patterns and by doing better with the resources we've already used, there is hope for our parks and Wilderness Areas. One would like to imagine that in the year 2029, the one hundredth anniversary of the establishment of Grand Teton National Park, the visitor to the Tetons will find it still a lovely and wild place; that through stabilized population and a tripling in size of the National Park System, the parks will be even less crowded than today; that such things as snowmobiles and speedboats will be no longer used in our parks because people will have discovered how wasteful and superfluous they are. One might also hope that Grand Teton National Park will have grown to nearly a million acres, which would include the Western Slopes, the Teton Corridor, and even a part of Teton Valley; and that land use and industrialization will have been sufficiently controlled to keep the surrounding region still beautiful and unspoiled.

Perhaps it is all best summed up by Margaret Murie, First Lady of American conservation and long-time Jackson Hole resident, in *Wapiti Wilderness*. "We shall go on with the little concerns of life," she writes, "but the mountains are still there, and now and then we may stop and look up. And if the valley itself can be cherished, there may be one 'golden age' after another—for our grandchildren and their grandchildren. Some of them may go to the moon, but perhaps the valley of the Tetons will still be a place of return and enchantment."

LEIGH LAKE

Two little girls lay giggling in a small mountain tent while a Teton thunderstorm raged overhead. Oblivious to any danger, they played a game of counting off the time interval between each bolt of lightning and the corresponding rumble of thunder. A few times there was no separation at all between the blinding flash and the deafening explosion, and each time I nervously scanned the lodgepole pine forest wondering what the likelihood was, out of the thousands of acres of forest, of lightning striking the trees we camped under. Despite my estimate of low probability, reassurance failed to come as crash after crash split the night sky. The drumming of rain on the tents was surpassed in loudness only by an occasional roar of thunder. It was a beautiful storm, and those two girls enjoyed every exciting minute of it.

Later in the evening the storm moved on to the east where it continued to rumble around the Gros Ventre Range. Unzipping the tent, I poked my head into a dripping darkness to discover that the clouds had cleared away leaving a bright, full moon to illuminate the landscape. Rain dripped slowly from the trees, with an occasional breeze triggering another downpour. The massive Tetons, so close here and bathed in cool light, stood dark against an incredible array of stars. As I looked about I spied the two little girls peering quietly out at the same scene. We exchanged glances but no words were spoken. The beauty of the land was communication enough.

One of those two girls was my own daughter Jean Anne, and Kim was the daughter of one of the two other families who had backpacked into Leigh Lake with us on that July weekend. As backpacking trips go, this one is pretty low pressure. It involves two, maybe three, miles over level terrain. Most of my mountain-climbing cronies look down their long noses at these annual Leigh Lake sojourns, and yet these trips have often been more enjoyable than many others we've made into more remote and rugged country. Perhaps it's because there is a chance to relax. Relax and learn something about a place. Too often I've returned from a climb or a long backpacking trip frustrated because there was too little time to spend in any one place. Here there are no schedules, no need to press on. Staying in the same spot for several days gives me a chance to absorb the country, feel its moods, and learn something about the life and land nearby. In that outside world, assaulted by unpleasant and jarring sights and sounds, we tend to build a shell around ourselves and turn off to various external stimuli. Here we can gradually dissolve that shell and let the external world seep into our pores.

The morning after that thunderstorm we awoke to a brilliant day. The forest shone with the residue of the night's rain and it had a fresh, earthy smell to it, the rich odor of decay and of life that springs anew. All traces of footsteps had been scrubbed from the sandy beach. We were the first people to leave tracks upon it. There was no other evidence of mankind about and we could have been living back a hundred years, when Leigh Lake was first described.

"Crossing this valley directly toward the mountain," wrote Frank Bradley, "we come at once to a series of high, steep, narrow ridges, covered with immense masses of granite and heavily timbered. Within the last of these concentric ridges, we come to a small lake, lying at the mouth of a deep cañon which runs far back into the mountains; . . .

"We have called this lake, which is about two miles long by a half mile wide, Leigh's Lake, after our guide, Richard Leigh (Beaver Dick)."

Beaver Dick Leigh was a holdover from the era of fur trappers who roamed this region in the 1830s. Most of them moved on when the market for beaver pelts declined, but some, like Leigh, remained because they liked the country. Those mountain men made little mention and gave no name to this lake in their own journals, but Bradley and Hayden gave official recognition to it and to numerous other features of the region.

Leigh is one of several lakes lying along the base of the Teton Range. It is second in size only to Jackson Lake (and about four times wider than Bradley's original estimate). It is also one of the deepest of the Jackson Hole lakes, a remnant left behind by the glaciers that once poured out of Leigh and Paintbrush Canyons. Lying snuggled against the southeast flank of Mount Moran, it has a deep-blue bay jutting to the west to catch the roaring stream now falling out of Leigh Canyon. It is one of the few valley lakes in Grand Teton National Park that is still roadless and wild.

"What do you *do* there?" people have asked, curious as to why we've returned summer after summer instead of moving on to new places. Watch. Listen. Perceive. You discover little things that might ordinarily slip by without notice. Important things, like the way sunlight slants through a lodgepole pine forest, the way dew forms glistening jewels on the outstretched fingers of a lupine leaf, or how, with curious grace, a small garter snake glides quietly through grass.

One of my more important discoveries is that this lake has a daily cycle, a series of moods that repeat. It isn't a changeless repetition, for no two days are ever quite the same, but over a period of time some patterns become noticeable.

With the earliest light of dawn the lake is a dark, cool mirror with a light mist sometimes hugging the surface, softening the reflections of the peaks. The mirror remains for some time, and as the brilliant sunlight creeps down the mountains the image becomes more intense. A strange phenomenon: waves seem reluctant to propagate upon the lake, almost as though there were some force keeping the surface stretched tightly. The disturbance made by an alighting gull is smoothed quickly into the mirror again.

When the sun rises high enough to light the water directly and the mist and low hanging clouds have dissipated, the lake seems to relax and the surface loses its specular finish. Gentle ripples erase the memory of reflected mountains. In protected coves and pockets along the shore remnants of the mirror remain for a while as the main body becomes a rough-textured blue, but soon a light breeze touches it all and the trees and grasses that stood motionless on the shore now pick up the rhythm of the wind and sway gently.

Then the mood changes quickly. By midmorning the water becomes a turbulent blue, a coarse, raspy face that catches the glint of sunshine on its rough surface. As morning gives way to afternoon the surface becomes even more choppy as wind spills from the peaks and out of the canyons. White-caps are now common, a warning to keep canoes close to shore. Small waves wash constantly onto the sandy beach, picking up bits of leaves or pine needles or pollen, throwing them onto the sand, then removing them again in an endless repetition. Late in the afternoon the lake is a massive glare, painful to look at, as sunlight pours down between the jagged clefts of the peaks and is refracted by the rippling, shimmering surface. By now the brisk wind has begun to subside and the water is again becoming quiet and calm.

Dusk returns Leigh Lake to a serenity that rivals dawn. As the sun goes down, clouds glow above the peaks. Cloudless days end with a luminous orange-yellow sky blending into blue some-where above the sharp silhouettes across the lake. This is the time of sounds, the haunting cry of a loon or the yapping of a coyote far away. The lake isn't completely subdued, for slow, gentle waves continue to roll up and expire tiredly on the sand. Only after dark does the water smooth itself into that mirror again, and when there is a moon you can once more see the reflected peaks on the dark surface.

The pattern, at times, seems changeless. But frequently that pattern is broken by storms, storms that have a predictability of their own. The day may begin like any other. Even the scattered flotilla of clouds drifting over at midmorning seems the same. By noon, the area of blue sky has diminished and the clouds have grown from simple cumuli to huge cumulo-nimbus, textured with great con-volutions. They have a heaviness and color to them that seems to warn of violence. Sometimes they lie in wait behind the range, gathering themselves for attack, with only their great tops showing ominously above the peaks. Occasionally a distant murmur of thunder drifts over the mountains.

An advance layer moves out to capture the sun and almost immediately the lake becomes calm. As the sun disappears a dark stillness fills the air and the big clouds begin to move across the range, their whiteness gone, blending into a dark, churning mass, their undersides colored a deep blue-black. The air is tense and carries an odor of rain.

Now the storm begins. Lightning flashes and thunder echoes among the peaks and canyons until it is difficult to separate each new explosion from the last. One by one the mountains are captured by the black veil of rain descending in graceful curves from the clouds. Calmness still prevails, but soon a light breeze warns of the advancing storm. The pulse quickens and there is a slight dryness to the mouth as the fury moves closer.

If the main body of the storm passes to the north or south, its movement can be traced by a sweeping curtain of rain held aloft on jagged legs of lightning. When it is headed straight toward you, the boundary is marked by churning water on the lake, a thin, white line advancing menacingly in front of a wall of blackness. A violent blast of wind and rain signals its arrival and a miniature ocean surf pounds the shoreline.

Drizzle is a word I've carried with me from my New England days. The dictionary defines it as a "light mistlike rain." I don't believe that it ever drizzles here in the Tetons. If it does, it must be rare. The rain from one of these summer storms is a pounding rain, drenching and soaking, splattering small craters in the sandy shore. The wind and rain scrub and purify the land, releasing the deep musky smell of earth and soil, the sharp resinous odor of pines, and the camphor of nearby sagebrush.

The peak of the storm may last for a half hour or more. Sometimes there is a temporary subsidence, giving false hope, only to be followed by another peak of violence. When the full force of the storm has moved on to the east the wind quickly dies, the rain gradually ceases, and a silence embraces the lake and forest once more. Dark clouds may remain overhead for a while, but toward early evening they shred apart to let the sky show through again. With amazing speed, they often vaporize and dissipate by the time darkness has set in.

Here on this east-shore beach of Leigh Lake the storms reach a special peak of fury that is rare in other parts of the valley and even unique to other sections of the lake itself. Each year we've been struck by at least one extremely violent storm accompanied by terrifying winds and waves. The wind, at times, seems on the verge of uprooting the amazingly supple lodgepoles lining the shore.

It wasn't until our third summer here that we discovered that the full violence was limited almost exclusively to this east-shore beach. One of our party began hiking out to String Lake during the peak of a storm and found that the south end of the lake was absolutely calm. The water was glassy smooth and the air so still you could hear the buzzing of mosquitoes. When he returned to our camp we were still being blasted by hurricane winds. Only then did we get a hint of the special conditions that prevail here. Perhaps someone more observant would have spotted the most obvious clue right away: the beach, this fine, white, sandy shore that we like so much because it is shallow enough for the children to swim and wade in. South of this spot, all the way to the south end of the lake, there are no comparable beaches. The shorelines are rocky, the lake bottom covered with rounded rocks.

A beach is built by waves washing sediment onto the shore, and waves are generated by wind. This section of shoreline, then, must be subjected to more persistent or more frequent winds than the rest of the lake shore. But why?

Across the lake, poised and pointed like some massive gun barrel at this east-shore beach, is the gaping mouth of Leigh Canyon. Penetrating deeply into the range, all the way to the divide, this massive rift siphons off bad weather at higher elevations, funneling storms and winds down its great length and shooting them across the lake to this side. A few miles south of Leigh is Paintbrush Canyon, cocked at a slightly different angle, but aimed in this same general direction. Together they form a double-barreled threat that greatly influences the weather and the ecology here. This knowledge has made these trips a bit more exciting (Teton roulette, someone called it), and I doubt that anyone would vote to change it, even if one could. Still, when those dark clouds begin to form way up there on the divide. . . .

I would like to report that the cumulative effect of all our Leigh Lake trips has been the discovery of some great cosmic truths giving us super insight into the natural world and man's relationship to it. They've done no such thing, of course. Occasionally, some serious questions linger, questions concerning the kind of civilization we've created. Here, detached and insulated from it all, there is a chance to reflect a little. Once away from the world of consumer products you begin to realize that most are pretty superfluous.

This is the place where we introduced our children to wilderness—at the time they were only months old. Will they be able to do the same with their own children someday? Or will the excitement of a Teton thunderstorm be lost in the din of civilization?

Sadly, our Leigh Lake trips have come to an end. It's a self-imposed exile, perhaps the result of what can be loosely termed ecological conscience. Each year the number of people using this east-shore beach had been increasing and the land seemed less and less resilient, less able to recover from the impact of more people. So we decided that we could no longer contribute to this deterioration. Now that the children are older, we've moved on to places more remote and more distant (and I might add that we are finding these increasingly crowded). But Leigh Lake has special meaning to all of us, perhaps best exemplified on a winter's night when either Jean Anne or Scott, for no apparent reason, says, "Do you remember that time at Leigh Lake when . . ."

We will go back sometime just for a visit, briefly, because, in the words of Donald Culross Peattie in *Flowering Earth:*

> For every man there is some spot on earth, I think, which he has pledged himself to return to, some day, because he was so happy there once. Even to long for it is holiday of a sort. These visits of revery may be all that he can pay it for years, perhaps until his shade is free to haunt where it pleases. But some are lucky; some get back, and find it, to every leaf and staunch old tree trunk, untouched by any alterations but the seasons.

THE GRAND

John Steinbeck called it the "hour of the pearl," that time between darkness and dawn. And it does have a jewel-like clarity, perhaps because the senses have been rested, dormant those past few hours.

From our camp here at nearly eleven thousand feet on the southeast flank of Grand Teton, everything is steeped in an icy blueness, sharp-edged, and clear. The forms of rock and snow are discernible below in Garnet Canyon, and Middle Teton's massive summit begins to lighten perceptibly from a sun that is still hours from dawning.

I stir in the sleeping bag, shivering from the cold. It was a restless night. Fatigued from the long trek yesterday, I tossed and turned all night, dozing only occasionally. The trip had been long and tiring; up the steep switchbacks of trail leading from Jackson Hole to Garnet Canyon, up the Canyon itself to Spalding Falls, and then the exhausting climb out of the gorge to Petzoldt's Caves, these rocks and recesses we are camped under. Four thousand vertical feet, roughly, from valley to here. And another three thousand to the summit of Grand. We had hoped to continue on to the Lower Saddle, the connecting ridge between Middle and Grand Tetons, but an ice storm the day before and continuing high winds hadn't made that barren expanse of tundra very appealing. Here, at least, we would be protected if the weather were to turn bad again.

Fatigue alone does not account for my restiveness, however. Anxiety and fear are a part of it, for as I lie here watching the stars fade, something nags at the fringe of memory, a feeling from the fitful sleep. What? A dream? Some dread, perhaps, lying at the edge of perception, something primeval, gene-deep; a fear of the darkness and the vastness and the unknown. Almost *déjà vu*—did I live this before in some cave before time?—but not quite. I let it go.

Jim Kerr rolls over, pokes his head out of the nylon and down womb, looks at the brightening sky. "Let's go," he says. "We've got to move."

I prepare breakfast from the warmth of my sleeping bag. The air is cold and my fingers numb as I lie there lighting the little butane stove. It's August, but you'd never know it here; summer comes late to the high country. Sometimes it doesn't come at all. Breakfast consists of oatmeal that tastes like mucilage, washed down with hot, soon-to-be-cold, chocolate. Neither is satisfying. Despite, or perhaps because of, my tiredness, I'm not hungry, but I'll need some fuel for the arduous climb, so I have a chocolate bar and some cashew nuts.

Art and George are up now, stumbling around in the semidarkness. In a short while we are all up, preparing the gear. It's strangely quiet, no birds, no wind. Only the faint, far away drone of some waterfall and the occasional clinking of pitons and carabiners being readied. I stuff rain poncho, parka, food, gloves, rappel sling into the rucksack. The rest of our equipment will be left here. The camera gear—twenty pounds of it. Should I take it all or leave it? Yes. No. Well, maybe. Finally deciding that I should take all of it, I begin strapping lens cases on my belt. Then, without warning, we're ready to go. No fanfare, just a few words from Jim and we begin, picking our way upward and across the steep boulder-strewn slope. Leaving camp we also leave behind the last of any trees, some gnarled and twisted limber pines that struggle to keep hold of the mountain. As we move on, little rivulets trickle across the gravel and under boulders, water that comes from the steep snowfields above and to our right on the upper slopes of Grand. Most of the slopes are out of sight from here—as is the summit, lost because of the steep angle of view. It's still dark, but now the summit of Middle Teton glows blood red, signaling a new day. The earth turns and the Tetons —and we—are pushed slowly into sunlight. We cross the boulder field below Middle Teton Glacier, picking our way carefully over house-sized rocks. Black chasms yawn between steps and the sound of rushing water echoes in their depths.

At the base of the headwall leading to the Lower Saddle we pause a moment to study the route. The scramble up the steep slope is eased a bit by a fixed steel cable which, though not totally necessary, saves some time.

As we stand on the Saddle the whole world opens up. The sun has caught up with us, drenching the short and stubbled grass with warmth. To the west the Western Slopes and Idaho shine in sunlight. Not a cloud in the sky from here to Oregon. We pause a few moments to have some gorp, an odd and variable climbing mixture comprised generally of raisins, chocolate, and nuts. Its chief value is, of course, energy; quick energy from the sugars in the chocolate and raisins, longer-term energy supply from the nuts. Climbing and hiking in the high country brings on incredible thirsts, as would be expected from the amount of energy and body fluids consumed. Part of it, I'm convinced, is psychological. Here there are thousands of streams and trickles, each sparkling clear and each begging to be sampled, and the water is incredibly delicious, palate-numbing and teeth-aching cold, only minutes from being snow.

Now the toughest part of the climb begins. The Lower Saddle slopes upward at an ever-increasing angle, leading to steep rocks and gullies which in turn lead to the Upper Saddle. Grand Teton, it turns out, is not a single peak. Its western spur is a few hundred feet lower than the main summit and separated from it by the Upper Saddle. The vertical distance from the Lower to the Upper Saddle is about two thousand feet, but our ascent is not by that route. After climbing about a third of the distance to the upper notch we will turn off and head for the Exum Ridge which forms the southwest flank of Grand Teton. From here, it seems almost overhead.

Jim is anxious to press on because we were late in getting started. His anxiety is justified. Summer in the Tetons brings thunderstorms that occur in early afternoon with great regularity. The standard climbing joke here is an admonishment to reach the summit before the 12:55 storm comes rumbling through. But it's no joke. A few years before I had been caught on the summit of Middle Teton in one of those ferocious Teton storms. Sleet was driven to painful velocities by hurricane winds. Visibility was nearly zero. Worst of all, as we huddled a few feet below the summit, unable to go anywhere else, the rocks hummed and crackled loudly with electricity. Having had such a close brush with lightning, I'm not anxious to repeat it. So we move on, entering semi-darkness again as we pass into the shadow of the Exum Ridge. After the taste of sunlight, everything seems doubly cold.

The route steepens. I follow Jim, scrambling up some gullies coated with loose rock and gravel. Some short pitches of rock climbing follow. A few are treacherously glazed with ice. I keep wondering when we'll use the ropes and pitons. Finally Jim pauses on the crest of a ridge and points out the rest of our route. It is my first, chilling look at the Exum Ridge.

The west face of the Exum Ridge is vertical, a wall of rock varying in height from eight hundred to twelve hundred feet, an impressive sight. Its main feature is a ledge that slashes across the face diagonally upward, from left to right from where we stand, and it seems to intersect the ridge crest. Named Wall Street by some wag, this ledge ends tantalizingly close to that crest at the highest point on the vertical face. To continue from ledge to crest involves what my demented climbing friends call an "interesting" traverse. Meaning that you can fall off very easily.

As I stand here with a knot of genuine panic in my stomach, I keep hoping that one of my friends will bring us all to our senses and call it off in favor of spending the rest of the day in a Jackson bar. No one does. And I'll be damned if I will. I scan the western sky for the merest shred of a cloud that I can call an incipient-thunderstorm-about-to-engulf-us-and-maybe-we'd-better-get-the-hell-outta-here-before-it-hits. Nothing. O.K., Kerr, lead us on. I feel like a condemned man.

We scramble down, across the steep snow-filled couloir descending from the Upper Saddle, and stand at the beginning of Wall Street. For the first time we rope up, Jim and I on one rope, Art and George on the other. Although Wall Street is actually wide enough at its beginning, it narrows rather quickly. Too quickly as far as I'm concerned. The upward slope of the ledge is steeper than it appeared from our view across the couloir.

We stop. The ledge is now about four feet wide, but just ahead it disappears. Actually, it doesn't *quite* vanish. The rocky shelf narrows and then moves under a bulge in the cliff, making it almost impossible to continue the traverse. Almost. That's the key—apparently it is *barely* possible, using the tips of your boots on the ledge and bending your body to the contour of the bulge, to inch along and around the corner to the big ledge on the ridge crest. On practice rocks the maneuver would be no sweat, but here a thousand feet of air cool your boot soles. And there are no handholds. It looks as though only a strong westerly wind can keep you on the mountain. In keeping with my usual luck, there is no wind today. Do I *really* want to do this? Before I can truthfully answer that, I'm involved in the preparations for the traverse.

We find a good belay spot, a niche in the wall where I can anchor myself by rope and sit comfortably, braced to stop a fall. Jim checks the rope, then hitches up his pants in an unconscious sign that he's ready. "On belay," I say a little weakly. My mouth is dry.

"Climbing," says Jim.

"Climb," say I. Damn dry taste again.

He scrambles up the narrowing ledge and pauses. Someone has left a piton and sling in place under the bulge of rock. Jim checks it, decides it's good, snaps a carabiner into it and the rope into the carabiner.

"Climbing," he says once again.

"Climb," I repeat, and automatically stiffen my legs to brace them. I pay out the rope smoothly from the coil, through my right hand, around my back, through my left hand to Jim.

He is on his hands and knees now, inching along that last bit of ledge. Reaching the place where the ledge slips under the bulge, he faces into the rock and slowly stands up, leaning slightly outward.

My right leg begins to tremble involuntarily and I discover that I had tensed all the muscles in bracing myself. I try to relax, but not too much. Nervous tremors still shake the leg.

Jim is suspended for a long time, inching slowly and coolly around the corner while poised over that tremendous exposure. Finally he moves around out of sight and the rope speeds up. I ease it out, tensed for any indication of a fall. And then it stops.

"Off belay," floats from around the corner.

"Belay is off," I reply.

Now it's my turn. I make my actions slow and deliberate, partly to delay, partly to steady the tremor that has spread from my leg to my hands. Art and George joke with me and there is some nervous laughter all around. Each of us is fighting his own secret battle with fear.

I slip on my rucksack and fasten the waist strap. Now tie into the rope—bowline on a coil around my waist. Normally I can do it in seconds, but now it seems like minutes before I get it tied. "O.K., Norton, let's do it."

"On belay," with reluctance.

"Belay is on," from way off.

"Up rope!" A moment's reprieve while the slack disappears around the corner. Then it tightens. Swallow. Pause. Glance over the edge. No, don't look. Deep breath.

"Climbing!" Dry, acid taste again.

"Climb," from another world.

I crouch and move forward slowly. The rock is cold and distant to the touch. I unsnap the carabiner and traverse some more. Now I'm on my hands and knees. Then my left shoulder touches rock. This is it. I have to stand up here. There's nothing on the right but air. A hell of a lot of air, and not much choice but to look down through it all from this position. Fear wells up, bitter-tasting, heart-pounding fright. But I also feel a strange sort of detachment, an observer gauging my own behavior. It's not solely the great height that frightens, I'm thinking, but the uncertainty of my reaction to it. Panic is the mother of disaster. Every move here has to be cool, rational. And with this realization comes confidence.

I turn slightly to face left, left hand high on the rock above, right hand still on the ledge with fingers curled over the brink. Now up. Slowly. I lean back as far as I dare to avoid the overhang, but a lens case on my belt catches the rock. Down into the crouch again to shift the case farther back. Then up again, slowly. But the case binds once more. And once more I'm back in the crouch. "Why didn't I leave this goddamn camera gear at camp?"

Again I move the case. Then once more I move upward. The case brushes the rock but slides past. Shift feet and face into the rock. I'm up.

Now what? Hang on, man. Except there is really nothing to hang on to. *Thin. Delicate.* More of those great climbing terms come to mind. *A delicate traverse.*

I inch along to my right, fighting back another wave of panic. Jim is keeping just the right amount of tension on the rope and it's reassuring.

It seems like hours that I'm spread-eagled on that ledge, hugging rock; then I'm around the corner and a smiling Jim Kerr says, "What took you so long?"

Standing on that broad ledge untying from the rope, I feel giddy, elated, exhausted. An adrenalin high. The taste of fear is bitter, but conquest of it is sweet. We belay Art, then George, around the corner; then we are ready to move on.

On the crest of the Exum Ridge, we are once again in sunlight and the climb has become something different. The rock is beautiful. The sky is beautiful. Art and George and Jim are beautiful. Still functioning under that last, hot, coursing jolt of adrenalin, I climb the crest above easily. Then it's a flat traverse to the base of a tower. Moving to the right we enter a long, narrow couloir, rotten in the bottom but better toward the top where some short but steep pitches make for some good climbing. The rock feels good, though my fingertips are sensitive because of the constant abrasion on rough surfaces. The price of soft living.

The climb begins to take on a dreamlike quality. Rock passes by in fluid motion beneath the hands and feet. Everything works, comes together nicely, as in the precise beauty of a ballet. The climb is an end in itself; the summit, an anticlimax. I even begin to dread the end when we stand on top.

Onward. Across some gentle slabs to the base of another couloir. This one is steep, but good, with a section of brilliant, white granite that is difficult. I lead the last pitch and as I sit belaying Jim I can see all the way down the couloir to the Middle Teton Glacier, cracked and corroded, three thousand feet below. The steep angle of rock, the warm sun, the high, cold air, all combine to produce a feeling closer to intoxication than fright. Some words come to mind. H. G. Wells:

> You can go through contemporary life fudging and evading, indulging and slacking, never really hungry nor frightened nor passionately stirred, your highest moment a mere sentimental orgasm, and your first real contact with primary and elemental necessities the sweat of your deathbed.

We are now at the base of the Friction Pitch. Jim leads, I belay. Well named, this pitch is tough, with more exposure. The rock is steep with no hand- or footholds, but the angle (thirty, forty degrees?) allows friction—boots and hands—with some roughness of rock to keep you on. Out of sight, Jim stops and I hear the ping-ping of a piton being driven. Two hits with the hammer and suddenly the piton arcs into sight through the air and clatters down the couloir below. An obscenity floats down from above, then the sound of another piton being driven. The rope moves on, slowly at first, then more quickly as the angle eases off above, and Jim moves faster. I follow, Jim belaying me from above. The lower section is difficult to get started on. In exasperation I clutch the piton for a handhold and discover that I can slide it out easily with one finger, a fact that I eagerly—and somewhat gleefully—divulge to Jim when I reach the top. He shrugs, smiles. "That was an inspirational piton," he says. The ultimate climbing trip, I'm thinking, the *psychological* belay. Just the mind. No rope, no hardware. Not ready for that yet, I tighten the nylon that ties us together.

Onward. Across the top of a black, rotten-looking couloir, across some smooth slabs of granite that dip away quickly into a horribly steep and snow-filled gulley. We move over the ridge crest across a broad, broken ledge and plunge into shadow. The rock is dark and gloomy, basalt perhaps, maybe gneiss, streaked with small, white veins. Up a slanting chimney, we emerge again into sunlight; then up sloping blocks and over the ridge crest. And there's the summit ahead.

There are no sounds but the wind. The summit is larger than I had visualized it, broken into blocks and boulders which are dotted in places with grey-green lichens—the only sign of life here. There are no grasses or flowers, but I have faith that not far away, perhaps on the south side of the summit block near the melting snowfields, there is a miniscule blossom or two of alpine forget-me-not or sky pilot clinging tenuously to the harsh mountain and reaching upward to drink in this brief, warm sunshine while it lasts. We too drink it in. The 12:55 storm will not materialize today, I decide. Low in the west are small scudding clouds skimming the horizon, but they represent no threat. Some wispy vapors pass by almost within reach of us. Otherwise the sky is clear and blue-black.

I have a curious mixture of feelings, mental and physical. Exhaustion—the adrenalin has worn off. Elation—I made it. Sadness—sweet anticipation is gone now, forever. And a little anxiety; after all, we still have to get *down* off this mountain.

The view is unreal. Surreal, perhaps. Below, Jackson Hole swims in a thin, blue, heat haze with the Snake River threaded across it in a silvery lacework. North is the mysterious Yellowstone country. Not the Yellowstone of the tourist, but an ocean of wilderness where wave upon green wave of forested mountains pitch and toss, with an occasional whitecap of snow and rock. South and southeast are the Wind River and Gros Ventre Ranges. The latter is serene and placid, the former stormy and rugged. West are the Lemhi and Lost River Ranges and the vast Snake River Plain in Idaho. Also to the west lie the checkerboard farmlands of Teton Valley. Closer is Table Mountain, where Jackson made his photographs a hundred years ago. To the east again, Taggart Lake is a mere hop, step, and a swan dive below—seven thousand feet below.

I had hoped, in a perverse sort of way, that the summit would be frightening, terrifying in its height above everything. It isn't. It's all too vast, the scale too large for the mind to grasp. In order to fear a height one has to have a sense of perspective, a comprehension of the distances involved. One has none here, and it is disappointing in a way.

There is disillusionment too: a small gully on the east side of the summit is nearly half filled with rusting tin cans and other debris. *Slobbus Americanus,* it seems, roams far and wide. The price, I suppose, for increasingly crowded wilderness. Crowded wilderness? The summit of Grand Teton? Impossible. But there it is in black and white: according to the summit register ten other people have been on the summit today. Make that twelve; two more climbers join us. Let's see, counting us that makes sixteen people on the summit today, in an area of roughly forty by forty feet. I make a mental calculation, find that sixteen people in an area of sixteen hundred square feet is equivalent to a population density of 280,000 people per square mile! *That's forty times the population density of Los Angeles.*

From the summit of Grand Teton you realize how small the Teton range is, how delicate and vulnerable and threatened is its wildness. Man presses in from all sides. The total length of the range is forty miles—I can see most of it from here. But it is narrow, and I could walk across its width on foot, from Jackson Hole to Idaho in one day (I must do that sometime) .

Sadly, it's time to leave. We pack up our gear, sign the summit register that is rolled up in the lightning-scarred brass tube. I take a last look around. It may be a long time before I'm back here again, if ever. A few more pictures, then I'm ready.

The descent is by way of the west flank; we pick our way over and around jumbled boulders and down some short chimneys toward the Upper Saddle. Before reaching the Saddle, however, we have to make a 120-foot rappel.

Once more a dry, acid taste in my mouth and the hot pulsing of adrenalin in my veins. I step into the rappel sling and grab the doubled rope. Two lengths of 120-foot nylon rope hanging over that cliff are heavy, and I tug to get enough slack to loop through the brake bar on the carabiner. Then I pull the rope around my hips and grip it firmly with my gloved right hand. Ready. Or am I? That tremor again in my right leg. Leaning back and turning slightly I can see only the upper forty feet of rope. The rest dangles below the lip, falling free for seventy feet or more. The bottom is not in sight. Instead, I'm looking down into the South Fork of Cascade Canyon nearly four thousand feet below.

After I step over the edge and begin the rappel, I feel curiously calm. Once committed there is no turning back. Might as well enjoy it. The rope hums through my gloves and the brake bar as I dance down the steep rock toward the lip of the final plunge. There I pause. For the first time I can see Art, who had gone first. The rock overhangs below here, and the rope, as I lean back, swings free in space. I take a deep breath, then ease over the lip, trying to avoid swinging in against the rock. Then I'm free, dangling on this delicate-looking umbilical cord that ties me to the mountain. As the rope sings by I begin to spin slowly and a gradual, almost psychedelic, panorama unfolds: granite, sky, clouds, Idaho, Cascade Canyon, granite again. And then I touch ground. The taut rope leaps up when I release it. The ends dangle six or eight feet above the ground. Only my weight stretched it enough to reach all the way.

We are standing at the Upper Saddle, about thirteen thousand feet high. When the others join us we start down the long, steep scramble to the Lower Saddle. Now there's just a tired numbness. Rock blends into rock. A hot sun blazes in the late-afternoon sky. The Lower Saddle. Move down the headwall. Stumble over the big boulders of the moraine. A pause back at camp for a snack and a cool drink. Then on with the heavy packs. Slip and curse our way down into Garnet Canyon, racing the sun as dark, pointed shadows creep across Jackson Hole below. In total darkness we stumble through the last few miles to the car.

As we turn off the road from Lupine Meadows onto the main highway, I strain for a last look at the mountains. It's totally black. The moon has yet to rise. The Grand looms darkly against the stars, more sensed than seen. Its summit is as remote and distant as ever. I've been there, I'm thinking. But there's no feeling of conquest. Did the climax come at the intense moment on the summit? Or will it spread out over a lifetime, played back bit by bit? What lasts? Not the details; they fade quickly. What stays is the intensity, the pause over space, the feel of sun-warmed rock, the smooth fluid movements on a tough pitch, the hot sun in a blue-violet sky, the friend sharing a rope. Most of all it is the feeling of being—pounding heart, lungs sucking air, soaking it all in through every pore—*aliveness*.

HIGH COUNTRY

August 3: Dawn. A dense fog fills the forest with greyness, leaving beads of moisture on grass and trees. The tall, slim lodgepoles reach up into the dark mist. Looks bad for our trip, but maybe the sun will burn it off by midmorning. We stumble on along the trail around Jenny Lake that leads to Hidden Falls, the only sounds the clumping of boots and the creaking of our bulging packs. The ghostlike form of a moose crosses the·trail ahead. He pauses to look at us while we, in heart-pounding, breath-holding silence, stand frozen. He moves on and so do we, after a prudent wait.

Above Hidden Falls the switchbacking trail leads us up into ever-brightening mist. Sure enough, by the time the trail levels out and starts into Cascade Canyon, we break out of the fog into brilliant sunshine. Below, the forest and Jenny Lake are still in a sea of cloud. Now the incredible peaks loom above, the pointed forms of Mount Teewinot, the Grand, Mount Owen, with all their bristling pinnacles steeped in early morning light. It's good to be back among old friends.

Midmorning. The heat, trapped between these soaring granite walls, becomes oppressive. Leaning under our heavy loads, we make our way slowly along the trail. There's no need to hurry. For the most part this section of Cascade Canyon is level, or nearly so. The stream meanders in grass- and tree-lined marshes. We spot two more moose. Always above are the peaks; five thousand feet to their summits from where we stand. Sunlight glares off the snowfields. Everywhere there is water, streams and trickles plunging down the steep flanks to join Cascade Creek. Between Owen and Teewinot, a long, silvery cascade, two, maybe three thousand feet in length. Out of Valhalla Canyon, another long ribbon of water. We pass several patches of creamy-white columbine, touched with blue, but the real wildflower spectaculars, we know, lie ahead in the high country.

Cascade Creek alternates between serenity and rage. As we move farther up the canyon the stream becomes less placid and more wild, more typically a mountain stream. Above the ponds and marshes it is a torrent, torn into foaming white by the granite boulders that try to constrain it.

Noon. At the forks of Cascade Canyon we rest, then continue on up the South Fork before pausing for lunch. Barbara has never been to Lake Solitude, the magnificent alpine lake tucked at the head of the North Fork of Cascade Canyon, and we wish for more time to visit it on this trip. But our footsteps take us farther away as we ascend the glacial stair steps in the South Fork.

For lunch we stop by the stream in the South Fork at a place where it roars through a notch in solid granite bedrock. It feels good to dump the pack and stretch out on grass. Just above us and to the right of the trail is an incredible rock garden. Brilliant colors wave in the breeze: yellow arnica, pink monkeyflowers, red Indian paintbrush, blue lupine, purple aster.

After lunch we poke around, climb some boulders, take a nap, explore some side streams, listen to a marmot, hunt for pikas, soak our feet in the icy stream, lie in the grass and watch white clouds race across the blue gash of sky caught between Grand Teton and Table Mountain.

Time for decision. Should we camp here? Move on a little more? Maybe even cross Hurricane Pass today and make camp in Alaska Basin? No need to press on, we have time. Ascending Hurricane Pass in the cool morning might be more comfortable. Agreed. Shall we stay here? Why not? Might be nicer farther on. Okay.

Shouldering the packs we move on, ascend another set of switchbacks, cross a flat, grassy meadow, walk through thinning forests of whitebark pine.

Evening. Camp is nearly directly under the towering east face of Table Mountain in a small meadow away from the trail. The main creek is still fifty yards away, down in a gully. We can hear it, but not see it. A small stream coming from the flanks of Table Mountain crosses the trail, passes near our camp.

From about four o'clock on our camp is in cold shadow as the sun has passed behind the walls above. Behind us looms the Grand Teton, foreshortened by the steep angle of view, its rough granite glowing warmly in the late-afternoon sunlight.

Supper is a freeze-dried meal cooked on a small butane stove, with no campfire, as firewood is scarce here near the fringe of the timberline. Besides, all dead wood should be left where it lies, for the process of decay is slow in the alpine climate, and every bit of humus and nutrient is vital to the tenuous plant life.

We pitch the small tent, picking a spot where the least amount of grass and flowers will be trampled. The sky is clear, so the tent is probably superfluous tonight. But better to pitch it now than in darkness during a sudden storm.

Sunset is subtle when you are camped in the confines of a deep gorge. The sky grows darker, of course. But there is no fiery splash of color, only the soft, lingering alpenglow on Grand Teton. And then darkness.

August 4: Morning. We are late getting up. It's difficult leaving the warm sleeping bag for the chilled morning air. It must have been below freezing last night, for small patches of water near the stream have a thin, delicate film of ice on them. And the grass has a crisp coating of frost.

While packing the gear after breakfast we watch a marmot who has let curiosity overcome his fear as he slowly makes his way toward our camping spot. He pauses on a rock, slides down, ambles to a tree, retreats a bit, tries another rock, finally creeps slowly, cautiously, through the grass to the spot where the tent had rested. The quick movement of lifting a pack frightens him and he streaks off, a rippling mass of golden fur, headed for the safety of his boulder-field home.

When we move on, our part of the gorge is still in deep shadow. In a mile or so the sun peers over the notch between Middle and Grand Tetons and we have to stop to peel off sweaters. This chilled land seems to breathe deeply the warming sunlight.

Noon. We are well above timberline now and the land is open, seemingly barren. Rocky soil, the pulverized remains of glaciation, supports clumps of short grass. Flowers grow everywhere, especially alongside the numerous little streams and trickles. It almost seems as though the flowers are an atonement for the sparsity of other vegetation.

We ascend the last few switchbacks to the top of Hurricane Pass and here pause for a good long while to take in the panorama. Spread in front of us is the main Teton Range; the Grand Teton is an almost perfect pyramid from this angle. To our right Schoolroom Glacier lies against the vertical limestone cliffs of the Wall, its snout emptying into a small, murky tarn, or lake. Although our elevation, 10,350 feet, is lower than much of the alpine country of the Colorado Rockies, this is true tundra. It is a harsh land. We have crossed several snowbanks on the trail here, so snow lies deep most of the year. The wind from Idaho that now cools us has a bite to it and we soon put on parkas.

The spot where we sit is precisely on the National Park boundary which runs north and south through here. Everything west, to Teton Valley, Idaho, is Targhee National Forest, meaning that there is no permanent protection for this quarter of a million acre part of the Teton Range. Roads and mines and logging have been proposed in various sections of these Western Slopes, places that are still as lovely and wild as when Jim Bridger and Jed Smith roamed them more than 140 years ago. We discuss the proposal we helped write several years ago asking the U.S. Forest Service to consider classifying these Western Slopes as a Wilderness Area for permanent protection. So far, the Forest Service has only studied it. There is fear that the agency will recommend only some temporary administrative classification. And in the meantime more destructive intrusions by motorbikes and snowmobiles take place each year. It should be more fully protected, perhaps as the William H. Jackson Wilderness Area, named after that pioneer photographer who first photographed the Tetons from the summit of Table Mountain. But wouldn't it be better to add this region to Grand Teton National Park so that the entire Teton Range would be protected in a unified park?

We move on over a small rise before dropping down into Alaska Basin, one of the jewels of the Western Slopes. There's Sunset Lake, deep blue in the midday sun. West of the glaciated basin are the abrupt sedimentary peaks of Mt. Meek, Mt. Bannon, and the sharp pyramid that several of us dubbed False Meek a few years ago for some obscure and now-forgotten reason. I can see the low saddle marking the end of Darby Canyon, a lovely spot with a superb view.

Midafternoon. The sun is really hot and shoulders ache under the foam-padded straps of our packs. But there is a nice kind of fatigue that has settled on us and there is no complaint.

Alaska Basin lives up to its reputation for wildflowers. It is, in fact, incredible. As we walk toward Sunset Lake we are hip deep in lush, colorful flowers: valerian, Queen Anne's lace, pink monkeyflowers, paintbrush. The carpet spreads for miles. By stream sides we find Parry's primrose. In other places the tundra is blue with lupine. Ahead, there is yellow paintbrush, marsh marigold, blue gentian, stonecrop, sky pilot, aster, penstemon. The mind boggles. Finally we simply run out of names; there are so many we can't identify. This is Barbara's first visit to Alaska Basin and she is enthralled with the beauty. I've been here several times before, yet each time the beauty of the flowers overwhelms me.

Early evening. We have decided to bypass Sunset Lake as a camping spot because of the huge, carnivorous mosquitoes. We pitch camp a mile or two south in the upper reaches of Alaska Basin, not as pretty a place as Sunset Lake, but pleasant and with a fine view of the main Western Slopes peaks. I had hoped for one of those spectacular sunsets behind Mounts Meek and Jedediah Smith, but low, grey clouds have moved in on us. This seems to be a frontal system rather than one of those typical brief-but-violent thunderstorms. Soon after supper we are shrouded in mist and a fine, light rain begins falling. No sunset and no stars tonight.

August 5: Dawn, so to speak. It has rained all night, a misty, drizzling rain that leaves everything soaked and saturated. Even the flowers droop under the load of moisture. We are glad for the tent. At breakfast we huddle in parkas and rain ponchos, looking for breaks in the dark mist surrounding us. There are none.

Once underway on the trail, the dampness and cold are tempered a little by body heat generated by exertion. We are reasonably comfortable—rain ponchos cover us and our packs, but I keep hoping for the storm to clear because the spectacular part of the trip is ahead.

Midmorning. The trail leaves Alaska Basin and skirts the base of Buck Mountain, ascending in switchbacks a precipitous wall to Static Peak Divide, almost eleven thousand feet high. We are in clouds and mist all the way, crossing patches of compacted snow which become treacherous because of the layer of water on them.

At Static Peak Divide I had hoped to show Barbara the splendorous view of Jackson Hole, over four thousand feet below. There is nothing but swirling mist. We are in the clouds; the visibility, at times, is only ten or twenty feet. A little farther on is the equally spectacular view down into Death Canyon, where the trail takes us down 3500 feet in three and a half miles. But this view too is lost. Still, the trip is not without its pleasures. It is eerie hiking in the clouds this way. It brings to mind, from time to time, imagined scenes right out of Tolkien's *Lord of the Rings.*

About a third of the way down into Death Canyon we break out of the clouds and see the canyon itself, green and lush below from the fresh rain. Low clouds swirl between the walls of the gorge, and while we look down on them they change shape and form. The stream in the bottom traces a serpentine path through forest and meadow. At the head of the canyon sits Fossil Mountain, craggy and crumbling, rousing pleasant memories of Darby Canyon and the Ice Cave that lie beyond. Continuing down the trail we pass through dripping forests of Douglas fir and Engelmann spruce. Soon we become as tired of walking downhill as we did of walking up; new sets of muscles begin to ache.

Midafternoon. We sit beneath immense spruce along the stream in the bottom of Death Canyon.

46

It is still overcast and an occasional light rain falls as we eat a snack of cheese and candy bars. The forest here is beautiful. In this weather, it is faintly reminiscent of the rain forests of the Cascades and the Olympics.

Despite the bad weather, we are sad that the trip is drawing to a close. On with the packs (how can they still weigh that much?); then we continue along the trail that leads through the narrow, vertical portals of Death Canyon, down the switchbacks that skirt the moraine of a phantom glacier that once spilled out of the canyon. The placid stream we sat beside moments ago is now a raging torrent, tumbling in great arcs as it leaps down the moraine to join Phelps Lake below. We pass through a forest of aspen trees that are the largest I've ever seen, grey-white and smooth-barked, where monkshood grows head high among thick, marshy undergrowth. We see numerous moose tracks along the trail, but no moose. Finally comes the agonizing ascent of the Phelps Lake Moraine. It's less than a mile of switchbacks, but at the end of a long trip it is a painful course. Too soon, we are back at the car sipping a cold beer and laying plans for the next trip, to Paintbrush Canyon and Lake Solitude; or maybe we should start from Hominy Peak and head over into Moose Basin in Webb Canyon; how about starting from Open Canyon to make a grand loop to Leigh Canyon, or—well, there's a long list.

4

6

7

8

10

11

12

13

14

15

16

20

21

22

26

27

25

31

30

32

39

41

40

43

42

44

47

48

49

52

56

57

58

60

67

68

66

72

76

77

78

79

80

Notes on the Plates

Teton Trails

I write this section with some trepidation. The wilderness of Grand Teton National Park, like that of other parks and preserves, is becoming more and more crowded, and I fear making it even more congested. I suppose many of us who are turned on and tuned in to the joys of wilderness country become rather possessive, if not outright selfish about it. I know I do at times. There are places, both in the Tetons and elsewhere, that I refuse to talk about or identify. I like my wilderness wild, meaning without other people.

On the other hand, I also recognize that only those who know and value wilderness will become staunch defenders of it. In the long term, the only solution to crowded wilderness is the establishment of many more—ten times, fifty times more—National Parks and Wilderness Areas. And to accomplish this goal will require many more people—including you and me—to fight for the preservation of more lands.

This section, then, is what my friend Bob Wenkam calls a guidebook with soul. The message? Tread lightly. It's all the wilderness we have right now.

TRANSPORTATION. Motorized vehicles of any sort are not allowed in Wilderness Areas or off the roads in National Parks. The only way to go is to walk. You see more, hear more, smell more of the country that way. Horses? It seems like a nice way to travel, but horses have much more impact on fragile alpine lands than do humans. If you care for the wilderness, walk. When you use modern, lightweight backpacking gear and foods and plan a trip wisely, walking with a pack isn't all that much strain.

116

FIRE. I frankly feel that campfires in most wilderness country are luxuries we can no longer afford. In many alpine sites firewood is virtually nonexistent these days because so many people have camped there. Dead wood has been scrounged and living trees stripped of branches, both serious disturbances to the land. Scars of old campfires circle many an alpine lake. Campfires do have an esthetic and traditional appeal. I like them too—but not at the expense of scarring the land and consuming scarce wood.

Small backpacking stoves—either butane or gasoline fueled—are much more efficient for cooking than a campfire, and efficiency is important here. I can cook several meals on one cartridge of my Bluet butane stove if I'm careful and frugal. Sitting in front of a little stove or burner does not provide the esthetic experience of sitting around a campfire. On the other hand, it *is* an esthetic experience to pack up your camp and discover that you've left little, if any, evidence of your having been there. That's the goal.

SHELTER. Forget the old Boy Scout lore of cutting saplings and building a lean-to. It isn't worth the effort, to say nothing of the damage it causes. Lightweight tarps and tents have become pretty inexpensive these days and provide excellent shelter. Plastic "tube" tents are really light and keep you dry during brief storms. Again, the goal is to minimize impact, so use some care when pitching the tent. Don't "trench" or dig ditches around the tent to divert rainwater. If you choose the proper place to camp, ditches are unnecessary, especially if the tent has a sewn-in floor. Of course, making the old bed of pine boughs is really pointless today; foam pads or air mattresses are much more comfortable.

LITTER. The rule here is: *if you can pack in any container full, you can sure as hell pack it out empty.* Don't bury any litter. It simply doesn't decay fast enough (aluminum foil and cans don't decay at all) , and when too many people bury trash, it creates incredible problems. Carry a plastic bag in your pack for empty cans, envelopes, etc.; and *pack it out.* While you're at it, it doesn't take much exertion to pack out a can or two that someone else has left behind.

SANITATION. As certain wilderness campsites become more crowded, the problem of human waste takes on serious proportions. In high alpine country human waste does not decay and become assimilated as rapidly as it does at lower altitudes. Human-waste pollution may become the major factor in determining carrying capacity and setting limitations on the numbers of people allowed in wildernesses. There is no easy solution, but a few precautions help. Choose a toilet site well away from streams and lakes, the farther the better. Dig a *small* hole—six inches deep is sufficient. Burn the toilet paper. Fill in the hole again, perhaps covering it with some small rocks. Sanitation also involves the disposal of uneaten food. *Don't* dump it in streams and lakes. Bury it, along with rinse and wash water. Use detergent (only a biodegradable variety) sparingly.

CONSCIENCE. Using the wilderness carries with it certain responsibilities for conservation. Much of the preserved wilderness country, Grand Teton National Park included, was hard won in fights with exploiters. Don't assume that, because we seem to be in an era of environmental awareness, all the battles are won. They aren't. If anything, preserving Wilderness Areas and National Parks is even tougher now because the opposition is organized and powerful.

So the message is simply this: join a conservation organization, be informed, speak up and speak out, write letters, lobby for parks and wilderness. There are numerous conservation organizations, but the following are hard-hitting and effective:

Friends of the Earth
529 Commercial Street
San Francisco, California 94111

National Wildlife Federation
1412 Sixteenth Street, N.W.
Washington, D.C. 20036

The Sierra Club
1050 Mills Tower
San Francisco, California 94104

The Wilderness Society
1901 Pennsylvania Avenue, N.W.
Washington, D.C. 20006

National Audubon Society
950 Third Avenue
New York, N.Y. 10022

National Parks and Conservation
Association
1701 Eighteenth Street, N.W.
Washington, D.C. 20009

Membership costs are reasonable, and even if you don't become active, simply joining contributes much-needed money to the cause.

EASTERN SLOPE TRAILS

Virtually all trails in the Tetons lie in and follow the major canyons. However, not all the canyons have trails in them. Inquiry at the Visitor Center, Grand Teton National Park, will give you more detailed information on trails and trail conditions. The hiking season is short in the high country. In early June there is still snow in Cascade Canyon, and by the Fourth of July Lake Solitude is normally still snow-covered and frozen. Some years, the Skyline Trail near Static Peak Divide is closed even in August because of heavy snow. So check conditions before leaving on a long trip.

Some excellent, detailed guidebooks are available. Among them are:

Teton Trails, by Bryan Harry (Grand Teton Natural History Association).
A Climber's Guide to the Teton Range, by Leigh Ortenburger (Sierra Club).
Bonney's Guide to Jackson Hole and Grand Teton National Park, by Orrin Bonney (Ord, Nebraska).

You should also purchase the 1:62,500 contour map of Grand Teton National Park at the Visitor Center.

Brief sketches of the hiking and backpacking possibilities in the Teton Range follow.

Webb Creek—Owl Creek—Berry Creek Region

This canyon complex drains the extreme northern Teton area where peaks are not as rugged as in the central portion of the range. However, this region is the wildest and most remote of the whole range. Elk are numerous and grizzly bear are occasionally reported.

The starting point for trails into these canyons is Berry Creek Ranger Station on the west shore of Jackson Lake almost due west of Lizard Point Campground. Easiest access is by boat across Jackson Lake. The upper ends of Owl and Berry Creeks and Webb Canyon are also accessible from the Western Slopes (see "Western Slopes Trails" below).

Colter Canyon–Waterfalls Canyon Area

There are three trail-less canyons that drain the Ranger Peak–Doane Peak area. All are accessible by boat across Jackson Lake, but they require some route-finding and bushwhacking once you are on foot. Of major interest is Waterfalls Canyon which contains the two most spectacular waterfalls in the park, Wilderness Falls and Columbine Cascade. Inquiry should be made at Park Headquarters Visitor Center for specific information.

Snowshoe Canyon

Theoretically, this canyon can be reached by the trail from String Lake that continues around the east shore of Leigh Lake to Moran Canyon. However, crossing Moran Creek, normally a raging torrent, is difficult and treacherous. Again, easiest access is by boat across Jackson Lake. There is no trail in Snowshoe Canyon. It is also possible to reach the upper end of the canyon from the Western Slopes by way of Dry Ridge Mountain, by making a traverse along the ridge northeast of that peak.

Moran Canyon

Moran is one of the larger canyons in the range, wild and trail-less and spectacular. Access to it can be gained by the trail around Leigh Lake and the east flank of Mount Moran. However, the crossing of Moran Creek plus the incredible bushwhacking involved make the trip up Moran Canyon from its mouth difficult. The best access to the upper end is by way of the Western Slopes, from Green Lake Basin. From there, it's a simple stroll from Green Lakes to the divide and down into the South Fork of Moran. The view from the divide is impressive; Moran is a big canyon.

Leigh Canyon

Beautiful, rugged, wild, and also without a formal trail, Leigh Canyon is reached by way of the trail around the east shore of Leigh Lake and the game trails around the north shore. Once in the canyon, some bushwhacking and route-finding is required, but the hike is not as difficult as in Moran Canyon. It also is possible to follow an old trail that branches to the right immediately after crossing the bridge spanning the north end of String Lake. The upper end of Leigh is easily accessible from Green Lakes or Granite Basin in the Western Slopes. Grizzly Lake is reached by dropping down from the Paintbrush Divide trail.

Paintbrush Canyon

This spectacular canyon empties, as does Leigh Canyon, into Leigh Lake. It has a developed trail and is one of the popular hiking trips in the park. From String Lake to Paintbrush Divide (elevation 10,650 feet) is a little more than 8 miles and the elevation gain is over 3700 feet. Paintbrush forms one part of a popular loop trip that continues from Paintbrush Divide and descends into the North Fork of Cascade Canyon, then returns to Jackson Hole by way of Cascade Canyon. The total distance is about 20 miles. Two days should be allowed, with a camp at either Holly Lake in Paintbrush Canyon or Lake Solitude in the North Fork of Cascade. Another popular backpacking option is to begin in Paintbrush, traverse to the North Fork of Cascade, then continue up the South Fork of Cascade and the Skyline Trail to Alaska Basin and Death Canyon, a distance of somewhat over 35 miles. Allow a minimum of three days; four is more comfortable. This trip takes you through the very heart of the Teton Range, but don't expect solitude. Because of the increasing popularity of backpacking in the Tetons, you'll meet lots of others on the trail and you'll be sharing campsites with many others.

Hanging Canyon

Lonely, wild, and remote, this small canyon is without a developed trail. To reach it you must traverse some steep hillsides on the east flank of Mount St. John, angling south and into the canyon. Leave the trail around the west side of String Lake where it crosses an open slope on Mount St. John. At Laurel Lake, a lovely little pond nestled several hundred feet above the trail, traverse south and upward, crossing some boulder fields. Bushwhacking is involved. Three beautiful lakes are in Hanging Canyon: Lake of the Crags, Ramshead Lake, and Arrowhead Pool. Surrounding you on all but the east side are towering pinnacles. A magnificent place.

Cascade Canyon

This is the center of hiking activity in the Teton Range. Cascade Canyon is easily accessible by trail around Jenny Lake to Hidden Falls, then up a few switchbacks and into the canyon. Once in the canyon the scenery is magnificent. The great peaks of the range—Grand and Owen and Teewinot —tower more than 5000 feet overhead. About 4 miles from its mouth, Cascade Canyon forks. The North Fork leads to Lake Solitude and Paintbrush Divide (see Paintbrush Canyon for loop trip). The South Fork is a portion of the Skyline Trail leading to Alaska Basin and Death Canyon. (It's about 20 miles from the forks of Cascade to Whitegrass Ranger Station, the end of the Skyline Trail trip.)

Because it is so accessible and so spectacular, on any summer's day there may be several hundred people hiking in Cascade Canyon. Generally, the farther you go the more the traffic thins out, but don't expect idyllic solitude on any trip in Cascade.

Glacier Gulch

Technically speaking, the Glacier Trail, beginning at Lupine Meadows (ask Park Service for directions), does not lead directly and easily to the Teton Glacier. Instead, after switchbacking up 3000 vertical feet in 5½ miles, the trail brings you to two lovely lakes: Surprise and Amphitheater. To reach the glacier requires a traverse across steep snowfields under the North Face of Disappointment Peak. It shouldn't be undertaken without the aid and the knowledge of how to use an ice axe. In one stretch a slip could be fatal. Once past this traverse, some tricky boulder hopping will take you up the moraine to the glacier itself lying tucked in the cirque below the north face of Grand Teton. It is impressive country; high above and around you are the soaring peaks of Grand, Mount Owen, Mount Teewinot, and numerous pinnacles. If you are not that ambitious or skilled a climber, Amphitheater and Surprise Lakes are excellent and beautiful destinations in themselves.

Garnet Canyon

This is one of my own favorite places, but it is becoming more and more crowded. There is no official trail in Garnet, but the canyon is reached by following the first 3½ miles of the Glacier Trail, then taking the left fork for another mile or so into the canyon. Here Middle Teton looms grandly above the end of the canyon, with steep walls boxing in the gorge north and south. In early season (to mid-July) the canyon floor is normally snow covered. Garnet is the jumping-off place for many popular climbs in the area; thus you are likely to run into many climbers or their base camps set up among the huge boulders along the stream in the canyon floor.

Avalanche Canyon

There are two beautiful lakes, Taminah and Snowdrift, located in this canyon, but there is no trail. Access is by way of the Lakes Trail which leads to Taggart and Bradley Lakes. Bushwhacking around either the north or south side of Taggart Lake leads to some marshes and heavier bushwhacking. Altogether, access is difficult. Snowdrift Lake is most easily reached via the South Fork of Cascade Canyon and following the old Skyline Trail to the Avalanche Canyon–Cascade Canyon Divide under the west flanks of South Teton.

Death Canyon

Although this canyon is well south of the main crystalline peaks, it has a spectacular beauty of its own. It has a developed trail, a part of the Skyline Trail system that connects, via Alaska Basin, with Cascade and Paintbrush Canyons to the north. The Death Canyon trail starts at the Whitegrass Ranger Station, off the Moose–Wilson Road (ask the Park Service for directions). The trail leads over and down a moraine past Phelps Lake, then switchbacks up into the steep, narrow mouth of the gorge. (At Phelps Lake the left fork leads to Open and Granite Canyons south of here.) Once in Death Canyon the trail divides; the right fork is part of the Skyline Trail and climbs the switchbacks to Static Peak, then goes on to Alaska Basin and Cascade Canyon. The main trail continues up to the head of the canyon, climbing to the Fox Creek Divide. Here you can follow the trail down Fox Creek to Teton Valley, Idaho, or turn left and go to Marion Lake and Open and Granite Canyons, or go right along the shelf below Fossil Mountain and Mounts Meek and Jedediah Smith to Alaska Basin and ultimately to the Skyline Trail again. It's all beautiful country, but again more and more people will be found on the trails.

Open and Granite Canyons

These two are lumped together because a single trail takes you into both. Beginning at Whitegrass Ranger Station, follow the trail to Death Canyon, taking the left fork at Phelps Lake. This trail leads into Open Canyon and then climbs Mount Hunt Divide (elevation 9700 feet) and drops into Granite Canyon. Again, this area is well south of the crystalline peaks, but it is spectacular and beautiful in its own way. Watch for bighorn sheep near Mount Hunt Divide. I've never seen them, but there is a small band that lives in this region.

WESTERN SLOPE TRAILS

While not as spectacular as the sheer eastern front of the range, the Western Slopes of the Tetons have a beauty of their own and often provide magnificent panoramas of the main range. Access to the Western Slopes is by way of Wyoming Highway 22 over Teton Pass, then Idaho Highway 33 through the towns of Victor and Driggs.

The Western Slopes lie in Targhee National Forest. Many feel that this 200,000-acre region should be added to Grand Teton National Park. The U.S. Forest Service has conducted a study on the suitability of classifying the land as a Wilderness Area under the National Wilderness Preservation System to protect it from further encroachment. The preliminary recommendation by the Forest Service is favorable, but there is a long way to go before the area is saved. If you hike here you might drop a line to your congressman and senators to let them know how you feel about preserving this part of the Tetons, either by adding it to Grand Teton National Park or by designating it a Wilderness Area. Send a copy of that letter to the Supervisor, Targhee National Forest, St. Anthony, Idaho.

In general, the trails in the Western Slopes are not as well defined or marked as they are in the park. A Forest Service map is available from Targhee National Forest at the above address. As on the eastern front, the trails here tend to follow major canyons, although the more gentle nature of some parts of these mountains allows for trails that follow ridges and cross open alpine meadows.

Hominy Creek–Conant Creek–Bitch Creek

South of the Ashton-Flagg Ranch Road between Yellowstone and Grand Teton National Parks is a spur road that leads to the summit of Hominy Peak. The road is very rough and the last few miles require four-wheel-drive vehicles. (Hopefully, the last several miles of this road will be closed and allowed to revert. It's an easy and pleasant hike—no need for vehicles.) From the top of Hominy Peak a trail heads east to the National Park boundary and then drops down into Berry Creek. In addition, the trail forks near the park boundary, and the right fork traverses south for several miles, around the head of Conant Creek to Conant Pass (a crossing point of the Teton Range for early fur trappers), and on to skirt the upper end of Bitch Creek, the area described by Owen Wister in *The Virginian*. It's wild country, and the trails (there are several spurs off the one described) are not well used; sometimes it is hard to follow them. Along this trail and crest system is access to the upper ends of Owl and Webb Canyons. This trail system and its spurs continue on south to Hidden Corral Basin in the South Fork of Bitch Creek, over Deadhorse Pass, and ultimately tie in with trails coming up Badger, and North and South Leigh Canyons. (See below.) Local inquiry at the Forest Service District Office in Driggs is advised before extensive travel in this section of the Western Slopes is attempted.

South Fork, Badger Creek

There is a trail in Badger Canyon, leading to Deadhorse Pass and South Bitch Creek. Perhaps the most scenic route to the head of Badger involves no trail at all. A dirt road east of the town of Felt follows the *North* Fork of Badger Creek for a way and eventually leads to a ridge above the *South* Fork of Badger where it ends. The trail up the canyon starts from this road about a mile before the end. Starting from the very end of the road, however, you can follow the ridge (with excellent views of Grand Teton across Green Lakes Basin) past Rammel Mountain, and eventually end up on Dry Ridge Mountain looking down into the North Fork of Moran Canyon. Bushwhacking is moderate. The view from Dry Ridge Mountain is superb: Grand and Owen and Teewinot to the southeast, the back side of Mount Moran to the east. It is possible to traverse the ridge northeast of Dry Ridge to the head of Snowshoe Canyon.

North Leigh Canyon

Off Idaho Highway 33 about 6 miles north of Driggs, follow road and signs that lead to North Leigh Canyon. At the road's end there is a trail leading to Green Lakes Basin and, ultimately, to Granite Basin. Both provide access to the upper ends of Moran and Leigh Canyons.

South Leigh Canyon

Follow the road off Highway 33 as described above for North Leigh Canyon. Continue straight east following signs to South Leigh. The trail up South Leigh is hard to follow at times, and after several miles, one branch leads to Granite Basin. The branch is not marked and not readily apparent. The forest and stream in South Leigh are beautiful.

Teton Canyon

This is the prime access point and most popular jumping-off place in the Western Slopes. There is a developed campground at the end of the road in Teton Canyon. From there two trails start. The first follows the North Fork of Teton Creek, climbing a beautiful glaciated basin, and ultimately leads to the summit of Table Mountain, the spot where William Henry Jackson made the famous, first photographs of the Tetons. The total distance is 7 miles, and the elevation gain is 4000 feet. Start early and allow all day for the round trip. Instead of climbing the summit of Table, you can traverse around the south side of the flat summit knob and out to a point east of it. Here you can curl your toes over the edge of rock and look down—straight down—2000 feet into the South Fork of Cascade Canyon. This is the precise spot where Jackson set up his bulky wet-plate cameras in 1872.

The second trail follows the South Fork of Teton Creek up into Alaska Basin. It is about 9 miles to the Skyline Trail. Four miles from the beginning, the trail branches, with the right fork ascending the Devil's Staircase to the Death Canyon Shelf Route. Either branch is beautiful, and the South Fork of Teton Creek is one of the prettiest streams in the Western Slopes.

Darby Canyon

About 3 miles south of Driggs a road heads east into Darby Canyon, past a Girl Scout camp. At the end of the road a trail climbs the South Fork of Darby to Wind Cave (3 miles), which is spectacular and has a waterfall tumbling out of it. The Ice Cave is a mile or so farther, but there is no marked trail. Ropes and climbing gear are needed for it.

Fox Canyon

The road ends at a quarry, and a trail starts there and climbs to the end of Fox Canyon to join the trail out of Death Canyon. A loop trip is possible, up Fox Canyon, following the Death Canyon Shelf to the South Fork of Teton Canyon, then out of Teton Canyon.

Moose Creek

From the road's end a trail winds through lovely forest, eventually, after about 7 miles, breaking out into a high basin. Some small lakes lie in this basin, and the trail connects with the trail out of Open and Granite Canyons.

Notes on the Photography

I guess I'm pretty casual in my approach to photography. I keep no records of technical data for pictures; everything like that seems so superfluous, because the final picture is the goal. How I arrived at it is immaterial. Furthermore, I do no preplanning or preconceiving of pictures before a trip; I don't tell myself that I want to come back with a particular type of photograph. That's a disastrous philosophy for wilderness photography because you spend so much time looking for those preconceived set-ups that you miss the real essence of wild country.

For equipment I prefer 2¼ single-lens reflexes. I'd love to use a view camera, but toting all that weight and bulk on a backpacking or climbing trip just doesn't appeal to me. I use 35mm single-lens reflexes for certain professional assignments, but I'm not terribly excited about that format. The 2¼ format is a nice compromise between 35mm and 4 × 5 with regard to weight of equipment and picture size.

My current outfit is a Rolleiflex SL 66, which I consider the ideal camera for nature photography with its tilting lens and interchangeable backs, lenses, and viewfinders. It is a dream to work with for close-ups because of the built-in bellows and close focusing ability.

On backpacking trips I carry the Rolleiflex, with its normal 80mm lens, slung around my neck. In some specially made cases on my belt I have extra lenses: 40mm, 150mm, and a 250mm. Also in belt cases are film, extra film magazines, filters, and cable releases. On the trail everything must be within easy reach. If I have to stop and take off the pack for a piece of gear, I find myself passing up too many pictures.

A tripod is indispensable. Sometimes I carry two, one a regular-size model, the other a small table-top variety that is useful for close-ups.

Film? Almost exclusively Ektachrome-X. I like the full, rich color saturation of this emulsion.

In low light or bad weather I switch to high speed Ektachrome.

Speaking of bad weather, I'd like to put in a good word for it. I think too many photographers make the mistake of putting away their cameras when the day becomes overcast or stormy. To me bad weather and storms are a part of the changing picture of the natural world. I like them. I like the mood and feeling of storms and of the changing light during them. There is an excitement and drama to storms, particularly in the Tetons. Tough on equipment? A little, but the wear and tear is not bad. I carry some plastic bags to keep cameras and lenses dry, plus a rain poncho for myself.

Another thing about overcast weather: it provides flat, soft lighting. In the forest in bright sunlight the contrast is often too great. Shadows are inky black with little detail, and highlights are often washed out. Overcast weather provides a nice soft light for flowers and foliage, allowing subtleties of color to come through. Direct sunlight on the same subjects frequently gives a quality of light I don't like, a harshness that works against me. For some scenes I sit around and wait for a cloud to cover the sun and give me the soft lighting I want. It takes patience.

Another important factor for good wilderness photography is time. My best photographs are made on trips when there is time to absorb some of the country, feel its moods and characteristics. If the guidebook says that a certain backpacking trip takes two days, I like to take three or more. A leisurely pace makes it possible to stop frequently to photograph flowers or streams or an infinite number of other exciting subjects.

Photographing mountains like the Tetons presents a few problems. The direct, overhead lighting of midday tends to produce flat, lifeless mountain scenics, because the overhead light does not produce shadows that mold and give form to the peaks, and during the heat of midday evaporation from snowfields produces a thin, subtle haze that tends to wash out details. Early morning light and late afternoon light give nice shadows and sculpture the rugged forms of the peaks adding dimension to pictures. And, of course, the warmer quality of light adds some subtle color as well.

Filters? I rarely use them. It seems as if I'm always dropping them in a stream or getting snow or dirt on them. I sometimes carry some gelatin CC filters for experimental color shifts, but I also shoot the same scene without them.

For exposures I have a firm rule: never put blind faith in a light meter. There is no *one* perfect exposure for a given scene. Subtle differences in lighting and color within a given picture can be brought out by varying the exposure. Therefore, I bracket exposures of almost every picture I make by varying one-half f-stop or more on either side of the indicated "ideal" exposure. It means I go through a lot of film, but it also means that I more frequently come back with pictures that satisfy me. For example, in making shots of a storm breaking up on Grand Teton, I exposed about two full rolls of film in a matter of moments, varying exposure and also getting different positions of the swirling clouds.

For this book I spent about six years, more or less, intensively making the photographs, and in that time I shot nearly six thousand transparencies. It seems like a lot, but in looking back now I feel as if I have barely scratched the surface of the Teton country.

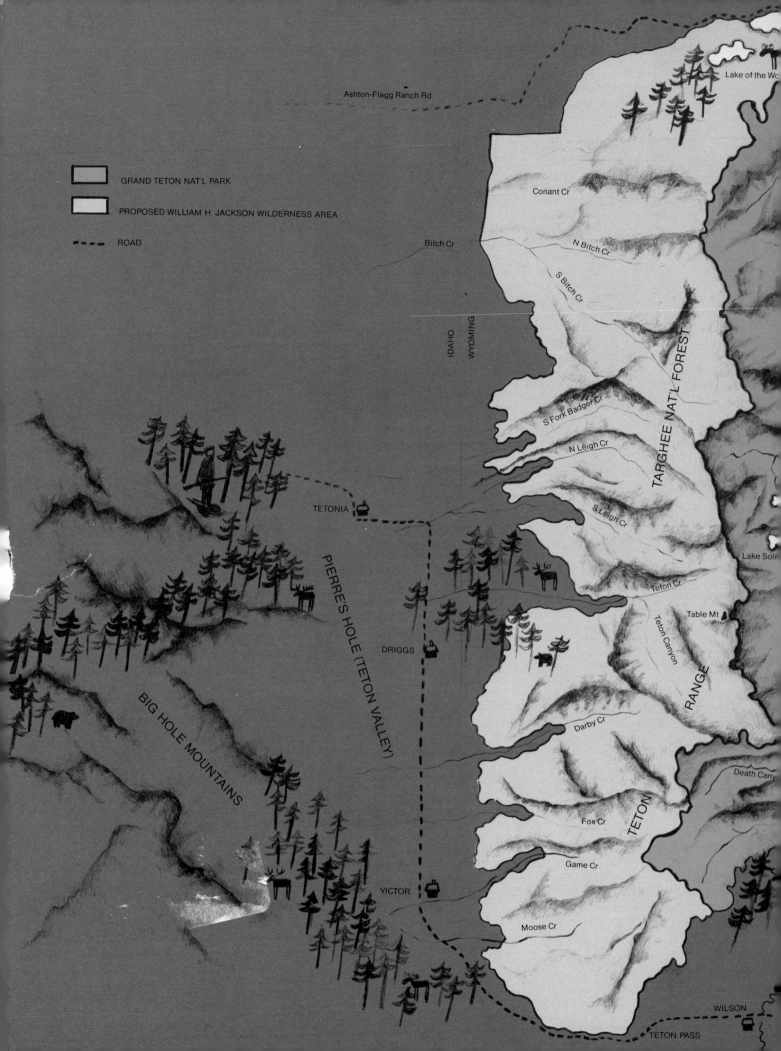

GRAND TETON NAT'L PARK

PROPOSED WILLIAM H. JACKSON WILDERNESS AREA

ROAD

Ashton-Flagg Ranch Rd

Lake of the Wc

Conant Cr

Bitch Cr

N Bitch Cr

S Bitch Cr

IDAHO

WYOMING

TARGHEE NAT'L FOREST

S Fork Badger Cr

N Leigh Cr

S Leigh Cr

Lake Soli

Teton Cr

Table Mt

TETONIA

PIERRE'S HOLE (TETON VALLEY)

Teton Canyon

RANGE

DRIGGS

BIG HOLE MOUNTAINS

Darby Cr

Death Cany

TETON

Fox Cr

Game Cr

VICTOR

Moose Cr

WILSON

TETON PASS